The State and the Self

Off the Fence: Morality, Politics and Society

The series is published in partnership with the Centre for Applied Philosophy, Politics & Ethics (CAPPE), University of Brighton.

Series editors:

Bob Brecher, Professor of Moral Philosophy, University of Brighton

Robin Dunford, Senior Lecturer in Globalisation and War, University of Brighton

Michael Neu, Senior Lecturer in Philosophy, Politics and Ethics, University of Brighton

Off the Fence presents short, sharply argued texts in applied moral and political philosophy, with an interdisciplinary focus. The series constitutes a source of arguments on the substantive problems that applied philosophers are concerned with: contemporary real-world issues relating to violence, human nature, justice, equality and democracy, self and society. The series demonstrates applied philosophy to be at once rigorous, relevant and accessible – philosophy-in-use.

Titles in the series:

The Right of Necessity: Moral Cosmopolitanism and Global Poverty, Alejandra Mancilla

Complicity: Criticism between Collaboration and Commitment, Thomas Docherty

The State and the Self: Identity and Identities, Maren Behrensen

Just Liberal Violence: Sweatshops, Torture, War, Michael Neu (forthcoming)

The State and the Self

Identity and Identities

Maren Behrensen

London • New York

Published by Rowman & Littlefield International Ltd
Unit A, Whitacre Mews, 26–34 Stannary Street, London SE11 4AB
www.rowmaninternational.com

Rowman & Littlefield International Ltd. is an affiliate of Rowman & Littlefield
4501 Forbes Boulevard, Suite 200, Lanham, Maryland 20706, USA
With additional offices in Boulder, New York, Toronto (Canada), and Plymouth (UK)
www.rowman.com

Copyright © 2017 by Maren Behrensen

All rights reserved. No part of this book may be reproduced in any form or by any electronic or mechanical means, including information storage and retrieval systems, without written permission from the publisher, except by a reviewer who may quote passages in a review.

British Library Cataloguing in Publication Data
A catalogue record for this book is available from the British Library

ISBN: HB 978-1-78348-579-6
PB 978-1-78348-580-2

Library of Congress Cataloging-in-Publication Data Available

ISBN: 978-1-78348-579-6 (cloth : alk. paper)
ISBN: 978-1-78348-580-2 (pbk. : alk. paper)
ISBN: 978-1-78348-581-9 (electronic)

∞™ The paper used in this publication meets the minimum requirements of American National Standard for Information Sciences – Permanence of Paper for Printed Library Materials, ANSI/NISO Z39.48–1992.

Printed in the United States of America

This is a song written by a much younger man than me who had the same social security number.
– John Darnielle of The Mountain Goats,
during a show at Bottom of the Hill, San Francisco, in March 2008.

Contents

Acknowledgements ix

1 The Metaphysics of Personal Identity 1
  1.1 The Curious Case of Benjaman Kyle 1
  1.2 The Primacy of the Practical 4
  1.3 The No-Self View 9
  1.4 Is Relation R Really What Matters? 12
  1.5 Three Separatist Solutions 14
    1.5.1 Lockeans 16
    1.5.2 Kantians 17
    1.5.3 Animalism 20
  1.6 Pronoun Magic 23

2 Narrativity and Normativity 31
  2.1 Identity as Social Reality 32
  2.2 Why Narrative? 34
  2.3 The Psychological Narrativity Thesis 37
  2.4 Forensic and Administrative Narratives 43
  2.5 Epistemic and Moral Concerns 45
  2.6 Exposing the Fraudsters 48
  2.7 Dehumanization and Depersonalization 53

3 Identity and Modern Statecraft 59
  3.1 'Seeing Like a State' 61
  3.2 The Personal Number 64
  3.3 Whose Power? 68
  3.4 Identities as Brands 71
  3.5 High Modernism and Postmodernism 74

4	Identity, Security and Trust	85
	4.1 Epistemic Gaps	87
	4.2 Trustworthy Identification	93
	4.3 Hypochondriac Identities	98
	4.4 The Mistrust Loop	101
5	Conclusion	115
Bibliography		121
Index		131
About the Author		133

Acknowledgements

The longer I worked on this book, the less complete it seemed. What I am about to submit now is, like any manuscript, an unfinished work – and I am certain that there are many ways in which it could be rewritten and improved. Yet the beauty of unfinished works is that others are invited to continue them. My hope is that this book will be such an invitation.

My sincere thanks go to Bob Brecher, whose patience, careful reading and constructive criticism kept my writing and my thinking honest and improved this work in countless ways. I am very grateful to the friends who have discussed the topics in this book with me over the years, challenging me and providing me with new cases and examples to think about; to the anonymous reviewers for Rowman & Littlefield who provided valuable feedback during an early stage of this project; and to Marianne Heimbach-Steins and to my colleagues at the Institute for Christian Social Ethics in Münster, who provided the best possible work environment in which to finish it.

Chapter 1

The Metaphysics of Personal Identity

In the early morning hours of 31 August 2004, a Burger King employee in Richmond Hill, Georgia, found a naked, unconscious man behind the restaurant's dumpster.[1] The man had several head injuries, his body was sunburnt and covered in ant bites, and he appeared to be in his late fifties or early sixties. He was nursed back to good physical health in the following weeks and months by hospitals and shelters, and a charity organization paid for eye surgery to remove cataracts that had left him blind.

But when the man had regained full consciousness, he could not remember who he was or what he had been doing in Georgia. He had no identity documents on him when he was found and he could remember only vague fragments of his previous life, with at least a twenty-year gap between what seemed like his memories of living in Indiana and Colorado and his reappearance in Richmond Hill. One of these vague fragments was the given name 'Benjaman' and so the man eventually adopted the name Benjaman Kyle, in part, because its initials corresponded to those of the case name assigned to him at the first hospital that had treated him: 'Burger King Unknown'. Although his injuries suggested an attack, local police never launched an official investigation into Kyle's case. The doctors and nurses who tended to him assumed that his inability to recall his identity and his history would be temporary. But Kyle's memory never returned. Three years later, he was diagnosed with severe retrograde amnesia.

1.1 THE CURIOUS CASE OF BENJAMAN KYLE

Kyle's story attracted local and national media interest in the United States. In 2008, he appeared on the *Dr. Phil* show in an attempt to find people who could remember him and tell him who he was. But this plea to reconstruct his identity was as unsuccessful as the FBI's efforts to find his fingerprints in their databases and to list him as a 'missing person' – although it was not his physical presence but his history that was missing. Unlike in standard missing person cases, Kyle's whereabouts were known but his official identity was unknown, and there were no traces of Kyle's former life that could be tied to his current self. In 2009, 'genealogical detective', Colleen Fitzpatrick, assembled a research team to uncover Kyle's genetic history. They worked on his case for years. Fitzpatrick's team narrowed the pool of Kyle's potential genetic relatives to two family names, but then Kyle suddenly broke off all contact with her – not unlike other instances in which he alienated those who attempted to help him.[2]

In 2011, John Wikstrom, then a film student at Florida State University, sought out Kyle to shoot a documentary about him. The short documentary, *Finding Benjaman*, became another plea for help.[3] When Wikstrom found Kyle, he was sleeping in a park in Jacksonville, living off donations and whatever little money he could earn under the counter. In the seven years since the incident in Richmond Hill, Kyle had been unable to re-establish an official identity. Authorities assumed that he had been registered *somewhere* in the United States under his former name and social security number, but because Kyle remembered neither and could not produce any other valid identification, they refused to issue a new identity. Without a social security number or any other form of official identity, he could not be lawfully employed, he could not access public resources such as libraries or schools, and he could not sign contracts and was thus unable to rent an apartment or buy a mobile phone. Even homeless shelters had turned him away.

Wikstrom's documentary, which played at several high-profile film festivals, reignited interest in the case. Due to the engagement of a Florida State Representative, Kyle was able to obtain a replacement identity card; a local restaurant owner in Jacksonville offered him a steady job and housing; and eventually another genealogist and television personality, CeCe Moore, took over Kyle's case, igniting a bitter rivalry between her and her former colleague, Colleen Fitzpatrick.[4] On 15 September 2015, almost exactly eleven years after he had been found unconscious behind that dumpster in Georgia, Benjaman Kyle announced on his Facebook profile that Moore's team found his genetic relatives and his former identity, thanking her and all the friends and charities who had supported him through the years.[5] Kyle had his social security number restored and new identity documents issued in his birth name on 21 September 2015, as reported in the *Orlando Sentinel* a day later.[6] For their article about the restoration of his official identity, the *Orlando Sentinel* chose the subtitle, 'Amnesia Stole His Identity for 11 Years'. But this seems plainly false: Benjaman Kyle had his identity returned to him *in spite of* his amnesia, and it was not the amnesia that had stolen it, but whoever or whatever caused the loss of his identity documents and made him fall through the cracks of American bureaucracy. He mused to journalist Matt Wolfe – who wrote a long feature story about Kyle's case in 2016 – that the main reason he had kept on searching for his history was not a desire to reconnect with his past but access to social security: his 'civil death' appeared much more threatening to him than his inability to remember.[7] In a literal sense, Kyle's identity was lost when it then proved impossible to find any official records of his existence prior to the attack. Indeed, one of the unsolved mysteries of the case is that, despite the fact that Kyle's birth name is known now, there is a span of more than twenty years during which there are no traces of Kyle's existence, neither under his birth name, nor his adopted name.[8]

Even the notion that it was hard genetic evidence that finally revealed his true identity is misleading: it was not the genetic evidence as such that did this, but the instrumental role it played in re-establishing connections to records of Kyle's former life. One of the most moving moments of Wikstrom's documentary is Kyle's reflection on the fact that for years, and despite all the media attention, no one had been missing him: 'When you think about it, it's pretty pathetic if there's no one that's actually looking for someone that disappeared.' It is this reflection that might also explain his initial reluctance to divulge information about his birth name or details about the genealogical research conducted by Fitzpatrick's and Moore's teams. He may have wondered what his old identity would be worth if there was no one to whom it mattered. Colleen Fitzpatrick once suggested that he shied away from having his mystery solved because it might uncover an unhappy past.[9]

Kyle has since re-connected with two surviving brothers and moved back to the city of his birth, Lafayette, Indiana – but he appears to keep to himself.[10] Over the years, he received plenty of attention as a medical curiosity, a bureaucratic anomaly and as a 'human interest' story. But why should his story be of philosophical interest? At first glance, it seems as if we have two separate themes to Kyle's ordeal, with at best a tragic but coincidental connection between them: One is the unusually severe and lasting amnesia; the other is the refusal of the authorities to provide him with a new official identity. The point can also be put in analogy to what the *Orlando Sentinel*'s headline suggests: One part of the story is about the brute physical facts of his identity; the other is about whether and how that identity is represented by official channels.

What I want to show, however, is that the connection between the two parts is much closer than what the given view suggests. The questions about Kyle's genetic relatives cannot be separated from the question of why no one came looking for him for such a long time; and both questions are obviously intertwined with the serious obstacles he faced without an official identity. Kyle's enthusiastic reaction to finally receiving a new identity card and his reflection on not being missed by anyone suggest that *what mattered* to him most was the fact that his identity was not recognized and remembered by anyone for eleven years. The identity rooted in the memories of his previous life and his upbringing was obliterated as much by the fact that no one came forward to identify him as by his amnesia – although the identity he created for himself as a response to this situation could not gain any official status, while it was recognized by new friends and acquaintances.

1.2 THE PRIMACY OF THE PRACTICAL

We might be tempted to ascribe the devastation of Kyle's identity to his inability to access his memories. In practical and moral terms, however, what seemed much more devastating *to him* was the lack and the loss of recognition, both personal and official, in the aftermath of his amnesia. Arguably, the authorities failed him in this regard. If my suspicion that the loss of his official identity had a greater impact on Kyle than his amnesia is correct, then this moral failure can teach us something about the nature of personal identity. They show that what matters for the continued existence of persons through time is not just their memory or the survival and the genetic history of their bodies. What matters just as much is that there are other persons *and institutions* that can 'hold them in their identity'[11] regardless of how their physical and mental lives might change. If we were not social creatures and as such dependent on rituals of identification and re-identification, metaphysical questions about identity would hardly matter. These questions become significant because our social lives are ordered around the notion that we have a unique and lasting identity as persons, which roughly overlaps with our physical existence.

Typically, issues of recognition have been relegated to the realm of *social identity*. And as one particular influential philosophical story suggests, social identity is quite different from personal identity. The concept of personal identity picks out the individual features that make you unique and tracks these features through time; and the standard metaphysical accounts of personal identity try to find such uniqueness either in the body or in memories and psychological coherence. The concept of social identity, on the other hand, picks out features that mark you as a member of a community: a family, a club, a church or a nation. These features do not make someone unique, they track similarities to other people. At first glance then, these social identities seem like very poor criteria of personal identity: something I share with other people is hardly something that could explain why and how I remain the same person over time. Michael Quante puts the point as follows: 'When we speak of . . . national or cultural "identity", then we do not mean numerical identity, but a kind of normative or evaluative concept shared by members of a social entity.'[12]

Yet supposedly unique and unchangeable bodily and psychological criteria of personal identity turn out to be fragile upon closer investigation. Many of the things that we might like to consider grounding features of our identity are in fact not. We forget things. Our bodies change radically over the course of a lifetime. When we pay close attention to our consciousness, focusing only on our 'inner self', it seems to disintegrate into a stream of randomly juxtaposed impressions. This disintegration was famously observed by David Hume, in his meditations on personal identity in the *Treatise*:

> For my part, when I enter most intimately into what I call *myself*, I always stumble on some particular perception or other, of heat or cold, light or shade, love or hatred, pain or pleasure. I never can catch *myself* at any time without a perception, and never can observe anything but the perception. . . . The mind is a kind of theatre, where several perceptions successively make their appearance; pass, re-pass, glide away, and mingle in an infinite variety of postures and situations.[13]

If you think about this issue as philosophers do, it might even turn out that there is no self, no coherent history and no identity. By far the most influential contemporary version of these 'no self' views was developed by the late Derek Parfit, in his monumental work *Reasons and Persons*, where he argues that 'identity is not what matters'.[14] He comes to this practical and moral conclusion from his metaphysical stance: for Parfit, there is no plausible metaphysical criterion for what constitutes the survival of a person that has the same logical qualities as identity. Since caring about identity is supposedly nothing more than caring about survival, we should not, in fact, care about whether we will remain self-identical beings.

Parfit shows that what matters in ordinary survival – which he defines as the continuity of mental and physical life[15] – can come in degrees and that it can branch – at least in science-fiction cases and thought experiments. I will discuss Parfit's view in more detail further, since it sets the stage for many discussions of personal identity in contemporary analytical philosophy. For now, I want to emphasize the crucial philosophical choice that frames Parfit's entire discussion of identity and survival. He thinks that our metaphysical view of identity and survival should inform our practical concerns. If there is no criterion of survival that fits the logical structure of identity, then we should adapt our practical concerns accordingly; if there is 'no further fact of identity', then we should worry less about ourselves and care more about others.[16] Parfit describes this as a liberation from the self:

> When I believed that my existence was . . . a further fact, I seemed imprisoned in myself. My life seemed like a glass tunnel, through which I was moving faster every year, and ta the end of which there was darkness. When I changed my view, the walls of my glass tunnel disappeared. I now live in the open air. There is still a difference between my life and the lives of other people. But the difference is less. Other people are closer.[17]

Yet the philosophical path Parfit chooses in *Reasons and Persons* – to go from a metaphysical 'no self' view to practical conclusions – can also be walked in the opposite direction. And that is what I will do here. Instead of assuming that there is a metaphysical truth that should inform our treatment of identity puzzles, I shall begin from how these puzzles are treated in practice and work from there to our metaphysical questions.[18] As the Benjaman Kyle case illustrates, philosophical puzzles about identity are entangled with social practices of recognition, both intimate and bureaucratic. And if I am right in my interpretation of Kyle's reaction to his ordeal, then these social practices matter a great deal more than metaphysicians like Parfit are willing to admit. These social practices can transcend the shifting natures of memory, mind and body, and thus offer a kind of stability that cannot be achieved by physical and psychological continuity alone. Parfit and his followers may dismiss this stability as pure fiction or as mere convention: my purpose here is to show that this dismissal is too quick.

If we begin with social practices of identification, then social identity does indeed matter for personal identity and survival – because *being recognized as the same person* over time matters. Being recognized as a friend, a family member or as a member of a larger community adds external stability to the changing nature of our minds and bodies. However, social identities are also fragile. People move; friendships fade; families and relationships break up. The pious become converts and apostates. Political allegiances shift. Communities change, merge and split into sub-cultures or are destroyed in political and social upheavals.

The modern nation-state was faced with the need to register stable identities in the face of massive cultural and social changes, and it had to fulfil this task without recourse to a universally agreed-upon metaphysical criterion of identity. It had to provide people with recognizable identities and, in response to this challenge, created administrative and legal facts, often seemingly *ex nihilo*. Modern bureaucracies have developed systems of identity management that transcend both the changeability of social ties and the changeability of individual bodily and mental features of individuals. These systems and their transnational interfaces make it possible to be recognized as the same person across different communities and countries. They make key points of your individual history legible to people who do not know you personally.[19] They map the rights and entitlements we have as citizens and travellers. But where these systems fail, as they did in the case of Benjaman Kyle, the result can be the loss of an identity that is recognized by others and, consequently, the loss of one's moral and social status. Kyle himself suggested that authorities might have offered more help to him, had he not seemed like a 'bum' to officers and clerks that dealt with his case.[20]

Those who fall through the cracks of these modern identity systems (refugees *sans papiers*, vagrants, terrorists, gender outlaws)[21] are hardly of interest to philosophers who think about the metaphysical nature of personal identity. They are the exception to the rules of 'normal' identity. But it is precisely these exceptions that offer a particularly clear view of the practical and the normative significance of personal identity. Those who fall through the cracks are studied by scholars who think about the nature of social identities: sociologists, criminologists, ethicists and scholars who work at the intersections of surveillance, migration and gender.[22] What I will suggest throughout this book is that these two largely separate traditions – of metaphysical reflection about identity on the one hand and of studying the concrete effects of making and unmaking identities on the other – can and should learn from one another. If they began with looking at concrete practices, metaphysicians would perhaps be less inclined to see identity puzzles as merely an intriguing philosophical exercise; and the descriptive work of ethnographers, sociologists and criminologists might gain if they looked at the practices they describe as an answer to a *philosophical question*.

To metaphysicians, thinking about identity documents and record-keeping may appear trivial. 'Surely,' they might say, 'a *sans papier*, a vagrant or a trans person who cannot get their gender noted correctly on a driver's licence – surely those people still *know* who they are. Their identities do not depend on what authorities choose or fail to recognize.' I am tempted to ask such metaphysicians whether they have ever been in a situation where their claims about who they are were met with official denial and rejection; and philosophically, I think that this attitude of dismissing practical concerns with identity management as trivial deprives us of potential insights about the nature of personal identity.

The metaphysicians who are looking for stable *criteria* of personal identity – or those who cheerfully announce that they cannot find any, like David Hume or Derek Parfit – are looking for a special kind of representation that corresponds to a special kind of fact. Hume says that introspection does not allow him to perceive an enduring self, since all he can see are shifting impressions. Parfit argues that what matters in identity does not matter for survival; and even survival might not matter all that much if we consider just how much our mental and physical lives change over time. From this lack of a stable and readily perceptible self that would ground a solid concern about identity, they conclude that this concern is misguided.

The possibility that neither Parfit nor Hume consider is that identity is not a *fact* but a *practice*; and that as a practice, it is a necessary condition of our mental, physical and social existence as persons. Immanuel Kant made this point against Hume regarding our cognitive lives, arguing that the 'I' that accompanies all our perceptions cannot itself be the object of cognition but is instead a necessary condition of all mental activity.[23] Some contemporary philosophers working in an analytic context have taken up the idea of identity as a practice and challenged the 'introspective' paradigm sketched above on its own terms; most prominently Marya Schechtman with her work on *narrative identity* and Hilde Lindemann in her *Holding and Letting Go*.[24] Both Schechtman's and Lindemann's approaches are inspirations for my own insofar as they define identity in terms of social recognition. I depart, however, from their focus on intimate familial and social contexts in which identities are constituted, maintained and undone or 'let go'; here, I am interested primarily in the role that official identities, backed by state authority, play in practices of recognition.

Schechtman's and Lindemann's work on intimate contexts highlights important aspects that metaphysicians too often overlook: How identities can be framed and fixed through name-giving and storytelling, and how such framing and fixing can be extended beyond the biological lifespan of human beings and beyond the loss of memory and ability. Benjaman Kyle can also serve as an example for this type of 'identity work', since maintaining his chosen identity depended on the goodwill of friends and acquaintances who recognized him by his adopted name. But the same case also shows the immense practical relevance of establishing and maintaining an official identity. All the goodwill of his friends was for a long time not enough to get Kyle recognized as a person in legal and administrative terms, that is, in terms that officials, doctors and potential employers, who did not know Kyle privately, could understand.

An official, state-sanctioned identity is needed to receive wages, to travel, to marry, to sign contracts, to vote and for many other basic functions of social life. In order to fulfil these functions, official identities need to manifest two essential aspects of personal identity: uniqueness and constancy. In light of this, it is actually quite baffling that metaphysicians have not yet paid more attention to the practices that go into the making and unmaking of official identities. Practices that control such essential aspects of our lives are worthy of philosophical attention and are not to be dismissed as trivial or as insignificant bureaucratic fictions.

Before we turn to the defence of my position that personal identity is, in part, constituted by administrative practices of identity management, I will discuss some contenders of this position: First, Derek Parfit's view that there is no self and that identity is not what matters; and second, views that distinguish different aspects of identity-talk and treat each as self-contained. Against these 'separatist' views, I will contend that we need a holistic understanding of personal identity in order to fully appreciate why social and administrative practices of identity management matter.

1.3 THE NO-SELF VIEW

In logical terms, identity is 'the relation that everything bears to itself and no other thing'.[25] Consequently, personal identity is the relation that a person bears to himself or herself and no other person. But this definition is merely an empty logical form; for it to become meaningful, we need to fill it with an understanding of what makes a person a person. Depending on the answer to that question, we can then formulate criteria for the persistence of persons through time as unique entities. This undertaking – formulating persistence conditions for persons – has, however, proven extraordinarily difficult, simply because there is no universally accepted account of what a person is.

From what I have said so far, it should be clear that my own preferred account of personhood is that of an officially recognized person – someone who exists on identity documents and in taxpayer records, for instance. Those who emphasize the intimate context of recognizing personhood, like Marya Schechtman and Hilde Lindemann, have a closely related answer: a person is constituted within a web of social practices. Schechtman, in line with my own views, emphasizes that 'the capacities and attributes of individual persons ... depend upon the existence of a social infrastructure'.[26] This answer would not satisfy the metaphysicians who are in the focus of this chapter, for the idea that personhood might be grounded in something that other people or institutions *do* is a mere distraction to them: when we want to figure out whether a thing or a person persists through time, factors that are external to thing or that person should not matter to the answer. 'Since personal identity has great significance, whether identity holds cannot depend on a trivial fact.'[27] Other people's beliefs or institutional pronouncements would certainly count as trivial in Parfit's view: whether I remain the same person cannot and should not depend on whether some clerk in some office thinks I do.

Parfit illustrates what he means by a trivial fact with a science-fiction case. He believes that what does matter is *Relation R*, a term he uses to refer to the psychological continuity, that is, the connections between different temporal instances of one mind. For instance, I am psychologically continuous with my younger self, because I remember some of the things this younger self did and experienced,[28] and I care about survival insofar as I want a future self to be able to remember some of things I am doing and experiencing now. But Parfit stresses that Relation R is not the same as identity:

> [Relation R] implies that [a teleported replica of me] on Mars will be me. But we might learn that my blueprint is also being beamed to Io, one of the satellites of Jupiter. We must then claim that it will be me who wakes up on Mars, and that I shall continue to exist if my blueprint is ignored by the scientists on Io. But if the scientists on Io later make another replica of me, when that replica wakes up I shall cease to exist. Though the people around me on Mars will not notice any change, at that moment a new person will come into existence in my brain and body. . . . As I have argued, what fundamentally matters is whether I shall be R-related to at least on future person. It is relatively trivial whether I shall also be R-related to some other person.[29]

What is the problem here? In order to answer this question, we need to spell out Parfit's view and its competitors in modern metaphysics. Parfit commits to a view that locates what matters about personhood in a *relation* between different psychological states. This relation can be weaker or stronger, and it can branch, as it does in the earlier discussed science-fiction case. Both of these features are incompatible with the logical form of identity.[30] First, identity as a logical form cannot be a matter of degree: something or someone is either identical with itself or it is not; it cannot be 'half-identical' with itself. Second, identity as a logical form must be transitive, that is, it must carry over between things that are identical with each other. If the morning star is the evening star, and if the evening star is the planet Venus, then the morning star is the planet Venus; if an elderly person in 2060 is identical to the author of this book, and if the author of this book is identical to a little girl in 1985; then the elderly person in 2060 must be identical to the girl in 1985. Relation R, however, is intransitive, as Parfit's science-fiction example shows: both the replica on Mars and the replica on Io are R-related to the original, but they are *not* R-related to one another. And so, neither is identical to the original, since at most one could be – but both are equally good candidates.[31]

We do not even need to employ science fiction to show how this is a problem. John Locke's account of personal identity, which was an inspiration for many contemporary accounts, including Parfit's, is often characterized as a memory-based account of identity,[32] for Locke held that 'as far as this consciousness can be extended backwards to any past Action or Thought, so far reaches the Identity of that *Person*'.[33] Hume's contemporary Thomas Reid already identified what looks like a fatal flaw in Locke's account: if identity were based in memory, then this would mean that in some cases someone 'may be, and at the same time not be, the person that did a particular action'.[34] Reid's problem was that we forget things and that our psychological connections to our earlier selves become weaker and can fade out over time. Reconsider the example I just used: if the elderly person in 2060 remembers how she wrote this book, and the author of this book remembers a visit to a bird sanctuary in 1985, but the elderly woman does *not* remember that visit, then Locke's account suggests an absurd conclusion: that the elderly person is me, and I am the young girl, but the elderly person is *not* the girl. The memory theory fails to reproduce the transitivity of the identity relation.

While Relation R avoids Reid's objection, because it consists of overlapping chains of psychological relations rather than direct memory connections,[35] the transitivity of identity is a challenge for any account that defines personhood in terms of a relation between different psychological or biological person-stages at different times. Any such relation could in principle branch, and any such relation admits of a gradual weakening or strengthening. In other words, no such relation is transitive, and no such relation is an all-or-nothing affair. *None of them* behave like the logical relation of identity does. If we defined personhood as biological continuity instead of psychological continuity – such that what mattered for survival were the connections between the different stages of a biological rather than a mental life – then Parfit's teleportation case would bring up the exact same problem: from one human animal, two were replicated, but at most one of these can be identical to the original.

The trouble with transitivity could be avoided, if persons were substances. If people were essentially souls[36] – immaterial substances – then personal identity would be grounded in the sameness of a soul that remains constant through all mental and bodily changes. But there is no good evidence for the existence of souls, nor will the body do as a substance: it might have an organizing principle – biological life – but the material stuff it is made of is much too variable and shifting to pass as a homogenous, self-identical entity.[37]

Parfit launches his no-self view from the following position: first, there is no good evidential support for defining personhood in terms of material or immaterial substances. So personhood must be defined as a psychological or biological relation through time. But any such relation is going to be intransitive – at least in fictional problem cases, like the teleportation case – and it undergoes gradual rather than categorical changes. Now, the teleportation case is supposed to bring out another intuition that is crucial for Parfit's argument: that the teleporter *accidentally* made an extra copy of the original should have no bearing on whether the original survives. But if survival is defined in terms of identity, it does – because the existence of the extra copy undermines the transitivity of identity. I would literally die if the machine accidentally made an extra copy of me – and this, says Parfit, is an absurd conclusion.[38] More formally, Parfit's argument can be reconstructed as follows:[39]

1) Relation R contains everything that matters in ordinary survival and ordinary personhood. But while identity is a transitive relation and does not admit of gradual changes, Relation R in intransitive and admits of gradual changes.
2) Since these relations are so different, only of them can capture what matters.
3) What matters should not depend on properties that are extrinsic to the relation between me and a future or past person.
4) Relation R depends solely on the intrinsic properties of the relation between me and a future or past person (the psychological continuity that holds between them). Identity sometimes depends on extrinsic properties (such as whether the teleporter malfunctions or not).
5) Therefore, Relation R is what really matters.

I will argue against both 1) and 3).

1.4 IS RELATION R REALLY WHAT MATTERS?

Let us consider one final science-fiction example – another teleportation mishap, which was storied in the television series *Star Trek: The Next Generation*. In Season 6, Episode 24, 'Second Chances', the USS Enterprise investigates a remote, inhospitable planet. On the planet's surface they discover an exact replica of the Enterprise's Commander, William T. Riker. The replica was stranded on the planet eight years ago, when a teleporter on Riker's previous starship accidentally created two copies, one of which returned safely to the ship and one of which was left on the planet unbeknownst to the ship's crew. Both Rikers return to the Enterprise and the replica joins the crew as Lieutenant Thomas Riker, using his military rank from eight years ago and William Riker's middle name. The two Rikers are not happy with the situation, however, and the episode's plot portrays their struggle to get to terms with what they clearly perceive as a threat to their identity: for instance, Commander Riker dislikes Lieutenant Riker's youthful recklessness, and Lieutenant Riker dislikes what he perceives as an adult satiety in Commander Riker. That their existence as distinct individuals matters to each Riker can also be seen from the fact that Lieutenant Riker takes the name Thomas in order to distinguish him from William Riker – illustrating how important the seemingly trivial act of naming can be. The conflicts between the two Rikers contradict Parfit's view that identity is not what matters – if that were true, they would have no reason to assert themselves as *distinct* individuals who nevertheless share many of the same memories and experiences. It would be enough that each of them carry on the life of young Riker as they see fit. But clearly this is not all that matters to them – Relation R is not enough. The episode's amicable conclusion is similar to the proposition that David Lewis makes for fission cases: that we should consider each product of a fission as R-related to the original and as identical to two people who already existed before the incident.[40] Lewis would say that both William and Thomas Riker existed before the teleporter accident – they just shared a body and a mind.

I suggested earlier that 'being recognized as the same person over time' is a valid criterion for personal identity. For our two Rikers, recognition matters because each is anxious to be perceived as an individual as opposed to a mere 'copy'. Parfit would likely dismiss recognition as a 'relatively trivial fact', and he might even admonish the two Rikers for their irrationality. But we need to ask: Is 'being recognized as' an irrational concern to have? In my summary of the Benjaman Kyle case, I already argued that 'being recognized as *someone*' was more important for the amnesia victim then the loss of his memories. To reframe the point in Parfit's terms: Kyle's survival – his actual survival – depended far less on Relation R than it depended on the actions of people around him who had the power to withhold or grant him legal identification, thus an opportunity to work and rent an apartment.[41] Let me now offer another example in the spirit of Parfit's teleportation case: Suppose I have an evil doppelgänger: someone who looks a lot like me has a voice very similar to mine and who can pass as me in most situations. Suppose this person has made it his or her goal to take over my life: my family, my friendships and my work. They have hired a detective to get all information they can about my habits and my history. They have hatched an elaborate plan to take control of all my identification documents. And one day, that plan comes to fruition and their identity theft is completed.[42]

Now we might brush off this hypothetical story by pointing out that identity theft is recognized as a grave criminal threat, which makes it unlikely that a comprehensive plan of the sort I just described would succeed. Or we might say that this identity theft is not really theft, for I still know who I am and what was stolen are merely representations of my identity. Yet consider how my life would change in the case of such a grand theft identity. I would lose the support of my family and friends. I would lose my job and my health insurance. I could no longer travel internationally. All of the things that require legal identification – many of which are crucial for modern life – I could no longer do. Taken together, these consequences are far from trivial, and it would indeed seem accurate to say that I had my life taken from me.

If this reading is correct, what does it show? First, it shows that Relation R – or any other relation of psychological or biological continuity you might put in its stead – does not contain everything that matters, thus disproving Parfit's claim 1). If it did contain everything that matters, I should not be disturbed by the consequences of identity theft. But the appropriate response to this prospect is moral outrage, not stoic indifference. What is more, in the scenario I described, the fact that I am still R-related to my earlier self counts for *nothing, if no one is willing to believe my claim that I am*. This observation gives us leverage against Parfit's claim 3) – that what matters should not depend on extrinsic properties of the relation between me and my past and future selves. That an evil doppelgänger decides to take over my life is surely an extrinsic property of the relation between me-before-the-crime and me-after-the-crime. But it makes all the difference to what my existence is actually like. If no one – no friend and no institution – is willing to recognize my claim that I am still me, then I have lost my identity in an entirely non-trivial and non-metaphorical way.

1.5 THREE SEPARATIST SOLUTIONS

So far, we have considered one sceptical view on personal identity, Parfit's position that 'identity does not matter'. This view stands in a tradition of analytical inquiry that seeks to separate questions of personal identity from other, similar questions. Starting from the observation that 'person' is a deeply ambiguous term, the analytical approach insists that we need to be clear about the different meanings of person before we can ask any fruitful questions about personal identity. This conceptual division lends itself to metaphysical questioning of a supposed connection between similar but different terms such as personhood, personality or personal identity. This metaphysical questioning, in turn, often leads to what I will call 'separatist' positions: for instance, the view that asking questions about personality or personhood is unimportant for, or even inimical to, figuring out personal identity.

Parfit's view is such a separatist theory: he posits that 'personhood' and 'personality' are about psychological states, consciousness and memory. From this starting position, he derives his view that personal histories – that is, the way that our consciousness stretches into our past via psychological connections – are not necessarily tied to the concept of identity, for these histories can at least in principle branch and merge, thus violate the logic of the identity relation; and from this metaphysical possibility, he concludes that our concern for ourselves is not actually about personal identity. Parfit constructs this line of argument by carefully separating the logic and metaphysics of identity from the metaphysics of personhood.

While I believe that the analytical approach of carefully sorting out ambiguities in the terms one seeks to understand before asking further questions is commendable, I do not think that this stance necessitates separatist conclusions about personhood: the different meanings of personhood might share intimate connections after all, and viewing them together rather than in separation might be necessary to fully appreciate the nuances of the term 'person'. In what follows, I will briefly sketch three different separatist approaches and then show how each leaves questions unanswered and offers an incomplete view of the matter. My analysis here builds on Marya Schechtman's work, who has attempted to challenge the analytical stance on personhood from within, and on Mühlhäusler's and Harré's linguistic study of the use of personal pronouns,[43] which, in turn, builds on Kant's and Wittgenstein's insights.

In the introduction to her most recent book, *Staying Alive*, Schechtman distinguishes five senses of 'person', which I will take as a scaffolding for my own argument against separatism: person as 'human animal', as 'moral agent', as 'rational, self-conscious subject', as 'possessor of particular rights' and as a 'being with a defined personality or character'.[44] These different senses of personhood quite obviously overlap in the case of what most of us would think of as a typical human person: someone who is an animal belonging to the species *Homo sapiens sapiens*, who is self-conscious and capable of rational deliberation, who has legal standing and is morally responsible for his or her actions and who has unique psychological traits. But it is easy to find examples of persons who lack one or more of these qualities: legal personhood depends on the political will to protect the rights it affords; corporate personhood is a legal construction and perhaps has moral implications as well – but it has nothing to do with humanity as a biological or psychological category; and humanity as a biological category presupposes neither rationality, nor moral agency, nor legal personhood – at most, it can provide the biological parameters of psychological personhood.

These different senses of personhood give rise to different understandings of identity, which, in turn, are relevant in rather different aspects of human life. Medical doctors care for human animals. Lawyers are concerned with the rights and obligations stemming from legal personhood. Ethicists care about moral agency, rationality and autonomy, but only some of them are also interested in psychology and law. Psychologists deal with defined personalities, but the biology and the morality of humans might not be of interest to them. Each of these groups also has a different investment in issues of personal identity: psychologists might try to uncover a 'true' kernel of their patient's personality. For a medical doctor, this would be of little or no interest; their task is the survival of the human body.[45] And the lawyer would typically be interested only in what records of their client exist, and not in their client's psychological states – criminal lawyers, for instance, are supposed to care about whether their client's alleged guilt is provable and not about whether their client is actually guilty.

The separatist looks at this diversity and suggests that our confusion about what personal identity consists in is really only confusion about which meaning of person is relevant for a philosophical analysis of identity conditions.[46] So the separatists either pick one meaning of the term as the one that provides answers to questions about identity, or they pick out another and declare that it had us accept false beliefs about the nature and the importance of identity.

1.5.1 Lockeans

John Locke wrote about personal identity in the *Essay Concerning Human Understanding*, because he had practical concerns in mind: he wanted to give an account of person as a 'forensic term', that is, a term denoting legal and moral responsibility.[47] In order to do so, he felt he needed to clear up the philosophical confusion around the concept of personal identity. In his general reflections on identity and diversity, Locke separates the concepts of substance, man and person[48] and argues that the identity of each consists in different things. While the identity of man – the human animal – consists in the 'same continued Life communicated to different Particles of Matter, as they happen successively to be united to that organiz'd living Body',[49] personal identity is grounded in consciousness and stretches as far back as conscious experience. For Locke, consciousness does not need to be attached to a single substance, nor to a single animal body. His fondness for thought experiments almost rivals Parfit's: he discusses the possibility that the consciousness of a prince could take over the body of a cobbler; that the consciousness of a human person might stay in a little finger that is being cut off from a body; or that someone might possess the soul of Socrates without possessing any of Socrates' conscious experience.[50] In each of these cases, continuity of consciousness is decisive: the cobbler becomes the prince; the little finger becomes the human person; but you cannot become Socrates by taking possession of his soul.

Locke's account of persons as self-conscious, thinking entities has inspired modern and contemporary accounts of personal identity that take their starting point from human experience and psychology but try to separate experience and psychology from both the physical features we have as human animals and from religious or quasi-religious beliefs in an enduring transcendental self. Parfit can be described as a Neo-Lockean in this sense; but even David Hume and Immanuel Kant – as different as their views on personal identity were – worked within the parameters established by Locke's reflections.

The Lockean and Neo-Lockean insistence on separating psychology from biology easily translates into a general scepticism about personal identity, as it did for Parfit and for David Hume: if you exclude the human animal from considerations of personal identity, you deprive yourself of one important source of continuity that could offer stability to the seemingly fleeting character of our mental lives. Locke himself, despite his interest in the moral and legal aspects of personhood, shies away from suggesting that his account of personal identity should inform legal practice directly. Mental states may be the true root of personal identity, but they are inaccessible to other people and institutions. So while insisting that waking Socrates should not be punished for the thoughts of sleeping Socrates,[51] he also admits that unity and identity of consciousness could never be *proven* in a court of law and that therefore judges are right to take bodily features as their primary criterion of identity and punish sleepwalkers or drunkards who claim not to remember their misdeeds.[52]

1.5.2 Kantians

Kant also believed that the human animal was of no metaphysical interest – and indeed nothing more than an impediment to morality. He engaged with Locke's and, especially, Hume's account of personal identity on their own terms, without challenging their neglect of the biological parameters of human personhood. In the *Critique of Pure Reason*, he offers an indirect response to Hume's scepticism about personal identity; a response that focuses on 'person' as a moral agent and a rational subject. The overarching project of the *Critique of Pure Reason* is to formulate the necessary conditions of the possibility of knowledge. This means that Kant also needs to consider the *limits* of knowledge. He distinguishes between the formal structure of knowledge and its empirical input and insists that the generation of new knowledge requires both: 'Thoughts without content are empty, intuitions without concepts are blind.'[53] Sensory input needs a conceptual framework to become intelligible, while a conceptual framework without any input cannot generate any new insights. The cornerstone of the conceptual framework – which for Kant is universal, innate and the structure of reason itself – is personal identity. But personal identity is merely a formal prerequisite of cognition:

> We are conscious . . . of the complete identity of the self in respect of all representations which can ever belong to our knowledge, as being a necessary condition of the possibility of all representation. For in me they can represent something only in so far as they belong with all others to one consciousness.[54]

If you could not consider yourself as a unified, enduring subject of cognition, in which all perceptions are processed as *your perceptions*, there would be no cognition, no thinking and no knowledge. In a sense, Kant repeats the

Lockean line that a person is a thinking thing – but he resists the suggestion that we can ever have any substantial knowledge of this thinking thing. 'I' is the subject of all cognition. But as such, it is a merely formal component of the structure of cognition and cannot provide any empirical input through which it might become an *object* of self-knowledge. 'No wonder', Kant might say to Hume, 'that you did not find anything resembling a self when you observed your fleeting perceptions: the "self" you were looking for made it possible for you to make these observations, but it does not provide any actual input'. The same goes for attempts to derive substantial knowledge about the self from the unity and identity of consciousness: 'The unity of consciousness . . . is here mistaken for an intuition of the subject as object, and the category of substance is then applied to it', such that the unity of consciousness appears like evidence of an enduring soul.[55] But this formal unity must not be taken as an object of perception and any inferences to a more substantial notion of personal identity are fallacious. Kant disabuses modern philosophy from Descartes to Hume of the notion that introspection suffices to solve the puzzles of the self, thereby relegating personal identity to the realm of notions – like God – of which we cannot have actual knowledge.

Interestingly, Kant believes that the concept of personal identity – just like the concept of God – can still be practically useful, although it is theoretically unknowable. In the sense of 'character', personal identity can elevate us above dead matter and our animal nature:

> Man, however, who knows all the rest of nature solely through his senses, knows himself through pure apperception [that is, the positing of an 'I']; and this, indeed, in acts and inner determinations which he cannot regard as impressions of the senses.[56]

How does this square with his earlier claim that the self cannot be an object of perception and knowledge? In the quoted passage, Kant grasps at a distinction that becomes the basis of his entire moral philosophy: he separates our status as rational beings from our status as human animals. As human animals, our knowledge depends on sensory input, and we cannot know anything about ourselves, our identity or our character in this way. But for practical purposes, these limitations do not matter: even though we are animals – and as such subject to laws of nature, bodily needs and contingent desires – as rational agents, we must consider ourselves free from these constraints. Morality for Kant is supposed to overcome our animal natures in the noble activity of moral self-legislation. And insofar as we are moral self-legislators – insofar as we can set rules of conduct (maxims) for ourselves that correspond to eternal laws – we must 'know' ourselves in the sense that we recognize the authority of something besides the natural world; something that is not need, fear, convenience or desire.[57] Christine Korsgaard, in her contemporary reading of Kant, puts the point as follows: 'to regard some movement of my mind or my body as *my action*, I must see it as an expression of my self as a whole, rather than as a product of some force that is at work *on* me or *in* me'.[58] And she continues, in the same spirit:

> in valuing ourselves as the bearers of practical identities, knowing, as we do, that these identities are contingent, we are also valuing ourselves as rational being. For by doing that we are endorsing a reason that arises from our rational nature – namely, our need to have reasons.[59]

For Kant and those who follow in his footsteps, personal identity is not matter of knowledge, it is a matter of commitment – be that a commitment to an eternal moral truth, as Kant suggests, or less ambitious, a commitment to 'some roles that we can fill with integrity and dedication'.[60] Kant's moral philosophy is too rich and too complex to discuss in any detail here, but I hope that this brief sketch shows what is *missing* from his account of personal identity. While it is conjoined with the practical aspects of personhood – the question 'Who am I?' becomes one with the question 'What are my obligations?' – it leaves out entirely the human animal. Kant dismisses the question of what *evidence* we could ever have of personal identity, and he turns Locke's forensic concerns with identity – the assignment of blame and praise – into a matter of rational self-disciplining. The price he pays for this move is the exclusion of all non-rational aspects of humanity from personhood. Those who are not yet or no longer rational beings are not considered persons, for they cannot yet or no longer partake in practices of holding themselves and each other responsible for their actions.

Rae Langton, in her paper, 'Duty and Desolation', shows how overly narrow this conception is by suggesting that moral indignation at another's misbehaviour can easily turn into pity or alarm at the recognition that the other person is cognitively impaired or temporarily incapacitated.[61] But this change in moral attitude does not necessitate that we see the other as a different person, or as a non-person. If my partner comes home late after a night of drinking with their buddies, and they are being fussy and unreasonable, my strategy will not be to engage with them in a rational discourse among equals. Rather, I will see to it that they drink a large glass of water and lie down, preferably without arguing. That does not imply, however, that I thereby see my partner as less than a person or a completely different person when they are drunk: they are the same person, only behaving differently – indeed, if they were not, we could not have a discussion about the incident the next day. What Kant's account is missing, then, is an understanding of the ways in which we can include even humans who are not yet fully rational, no longer rational or temporarily irrational in our social practices *as persons*.

1.5.3 Animalism

The third type of separatism I want to discuss is animalism. Here I have to contend with the fact that its main proponent in the Anglophone world, Eric Olson, does not actually think of it as a rival to other theories of personal identity; indeed, he is entirely uninterested in the question of what a person is and how it persists through time;[62] and he allows that some persons might not be animals (angels or artificial intelligences) and that some human beings might not be persons.[63] Olson's claim is simply that 'we' – human beings – are animals; and he finds this view to be much simpler and to have more explanatory power than personhood views that seek to locate humanity in some immaterial qualities, such as consciousness. He, too, follows Locke, but only in the sense that he accepts his definition of life: 'a self-organizing event that maintains the organism's complex internal structure'.[64]

Applied to cases of humans who are not yet or no longer rational, which were left out in the Kantian account we just discussed, Olson's view does indeed close some obvious gaps. Take the story of a human life: from infancy, to adulthood, and then on to old age and the gradual loss of mental faculties to dementia. The life is *one life*, but the Lockean and Kantian views of personhood as consciousness would seem to deny this: A person in the sense of a conscious agent is only there from late infancy until dementia destroys the mental faculties, and the view that persons are consciousnesses cannot explain why we would nevertheless regard these different stages of consciousness as an integral part of one human life.

Olson's solution – to care only about what *we* are, not what persons are – is quite elegant and seems easily to do away with the puzzles of personhood that concerned us in the first part of this chapter. Among other things, it fits nicely with the professional attitudes of surgeons and most other doctors, whose primary task is the survival of the human animal. But like these professional attitudes, it overlooks some things that are actually crucial to what we are. In order to show why this is, I will briefly turn to Michael Quante's account of the 'social nature of personal identity'.[65] Quante, like virtually all other analytic philosophers, is very careful to distinguish *numerical* from *qualitative* identity. He then formulates four different philosophical problems about personal identity, only one of which is directly related to issues of identity over time:[66]

1) The 'Conditions-of-Personhood-Problem' (e.g., when does a human foetus or infant become a person, can some animals be persons)
2) The 'Unity-of-Person-Problem' (e.g., when do psychological disorders interfere with our common sense understanding that one person inhabits one adult human body)

3) The 'Persistence-of-Person-Problem' (this is the problem of identity proper)
4) The 'Structure-of-Personality-Problem' (e.g., what are the different ways in which persons assert themselves as persons across different social and moral contexts; this is particularly interesting for the psychological literature on personhood and identity)

Now while Quante gives an account of the social nature of personal identity, he means by that only the conditions of personhood and the structure of personality. He denies, however, that either one could tell us anything interesting about the persistence problem and claims that we 'should give up the idea that we can solve the four problems by means of one single approach'.[67] Echoing Parfit, he admits that 'persistence conditions of human persons . . . should not be arbitrary or depend on social practices and shared values [or] linguistic conventions'.[68] Yet he resists Parfit's conclusion that thinking about identity in terms of persistence conditions is a hopeless undertaking. Rather, he urges us to distinguish questions about the social realities that undergird our talk about when and how someone is a person *at a given point in time* from questions about whether that person has existed as the *same person through time*. Like Olson, Quante insists that persistence conditions are to be formulated in 'natural-kind terms' and 'to be discovered by biology'[69] – that is, they are descriptors of the human animal rather than a human person. Conditions of personhood and descriptions of personalities, on the other hand, are properly formulated in social-kind terms. Yet these social-kind terms do 'not deliver persistence conditions'.[70]

Consider again our initial example in this section: an elderly woman is suffering from dementia. Suppose that the illness has progressed and she no longer recognizes her surroundings, nor her family and friends; she cannot speak anymore and she needs assistance with even the most basic tasks. The most urgent moral questions in such cases are likely to revolve around how much of a personality the elderly woman can still express – for instance, can she still signal her comfort and discomfort to the nurses? – and if she cannot, what, if anything, is to be done about that? Such questions have an obvious connection to the necessary conditions of personhood: if the elderly woman cannot express her preferences anymore, does that imply that nurses and other staff can simply treat her like someone who does not have preferences – that is, would they be justified in treating her *less than a person*? The answers to these questions are obviously formulated in 'social-kind terms' – in the sense that they need to be worked out in a social and moral dialogue and cannot be settled by an appeal to 'scientific facts'.

Now Quante and Olson might say that this is as it should be, but that questions about whether the elderly woman is still the same person as a healthy young woman with the same name is misplaced and misleading. In order to figure out how the dementia patient should be treated in a care institution, we do not need to know anything about persistence conditions – it is irrelevant whether and to what extent a certain personality has endured in the patient. Persistence would and should be settled by an appeal to 'scientific facts': either the dementia patient is still alive, or she is not. This solution – to decouple questions of persistence form questions of personhood in order to avoid all the messy metaphysical and psychological debates about identity – is as elegant as it is naïve.

For starters, in real-life cases of dementia, the decent treatment of the patient might actually hinge on whether the staff can see the dementia patient as someone with a history – that is, as more than a mere body – even though the patient has irrevocably lost that history. If they can, chances are that they would treat them more kindly and patiently – more like a fellow human person, less like a mere human animal.[71] In addition to these concrete practical concerns, Quante's account suffers from a false dichotomy of 'soft' social facts and 'hard' natural sciences. He writes that 'being a person, taking responsibility, or demanding respect for one's personality are possible only in a social world constituted by social rules',[72] apparently unaware of the long history of the use of pseudo-scientific categories to strip people of those attributes of personhood that provided them with legal and moral protection. Slavery, for instance, was a social institution, but the justification of slavery often appealed to racist pseudo-science in an attempt to show that the slaves were biologically inferior to the slaveholders and could thus be mistreated with moral and legal impunity. Modern history is rife with examples of pseudo-scientific justifications for social segregation, oppression and even genocide, and in this context, science is not nearly as hard and social customs not nearly as soft as Quante suggests.

He might reply that what is at stake for him is not pseudo-science but the supposedly objective truths of proper science, freed from any particular social agenda. But even this is misleading if what we want is a strict separation of the human person from the human animal. It is far from clear that the social sciences *must* strive towards some objective truth in order to deliver something that may count as 'hard facts' in the present discussion about personhood. Social sciences describe social processes, and these processes depend on history, geography and social standing. That does not make these social practices any less factual or less relevant for our present discussion, however. If I can adequately describe how modern societies have approached the task of recording their members' identities, then this is a relevant social fact that merits discussion – or so I will argue.

Here I want to note what the animalist account is missing: namely, an understanding of the social nuances of personhood. The criminal might be identified by animal features (their fingerprints), but the extent of their guilt can only be determined through an appraisal of their personality. Young children need lots of physical contact from their caretakers to develop properly; they require assistance and encouragement and patience, but they are also sometimes addressed as if they were fully rational persons – not because they are, but because their caretakers want to prepare them for becoming one.[73] Institutions commit a moral wrong when they treat elderly dementia patients as merely a body to be stored somewhere – even if the patient is past the point where they can express any disapproval about such treatment. In each of these cases, insisting on separatism about the different meanings of personhood would be to miss out on the complexity on what is at stake in the corresponding social practices. In order to flourish, human beings need to be acknowledged as human animals – like other animals, they need warmth and comfort from their caretakers when they are small and enjoy physical contact as adults – and as (prospective) rational agents and as unique personalities. There is nothing surprising or philosophically misleading about saying that personhood consists in all of these things, viewed together – it inhabits the space where different social practices of caring, naming, telling stories and holding responsible overlap.

1.6 PRONOUN MAGIC

To wrap up this chapter, I want to briefly present a linguistic study that attempted to solve the riddles of personal identity by analysing the use of pronouns, in a way that is directly relevant to the argument I presented so far. In 1990, Peter Mühlhäusler and Rom Harré published their study *Pronouns and People*, in which an entire chapter is devoted to the philosophy of language of the pronoun 'I'.[74] Their philosophical position is inspired by Parfit, Kant and Wittgenstein and it bears obvious similarities to Peter Strawson's 'descriptive metaphysics' of personhood[75] – and like these thinkers, Mühlhäusler and Harré deny that there is a substantive self, or soul, which we could observe in language use. 'I' does not refer to any content, it does not denote anything – but it is easy to *believe* that there is some mysterious referent behind the pronoun. This is, in a nutshell, the position they ascribe to Descartes: through his methodical doubt, he claimed to have uncovered the substance of the thinking self, the *cogito*, the one thing whose existence he could not, in principle, doubt.[76] But Kant might say: 'You took the formal requirement of forming a sceptical belief – that it be *your belief* – as *evidence* for the existence of a mental substance.' And Wittgenstein might say: 'You were fooled by the rules of grammar into thinking that behind these rules, there lay some deeper truth about selfhood.'[77] As linguists Mühlhäusler and Harré point out that went wrong with Descartes' method was that he took the *cogito* to denote an independent truth about him (that he is a thinking substance) when all it did was to index his location in geographical and social space. They consider all first-person expressions as double indexicals that mark the speaker's position in time and space, as an embodied person, and the speaker's social and moral positioning in regard to his or her utterance.[78] Let us consider 'I love you' as a simple example: when whispered tenderly and in private, the 'I' marks both the speaker's location as an embodied person ('*this* embodied person sexually and romantically desires you') as well as the fact that the speaker feels comfortable enough to express his or her affection this directly (perhaps it was the first time they said it, after weeks of being unsure whether there was enough intimacy and affection yet to speak of love). What the 'I' does *not* do, according to the thesis of double indexicality, is to imply some comprehensive report about the speaker's romantic qualities, or to entail a promise that the affection they feel will be permanent. That is, the 'I' in 'I love you' does not *denote* any additional information about the speaker.

This thesis of double indexicality can be used to disentangle some of the confusions about personal identity we have touched upon here; and it can be used to refute separatism about personhood. Mühlhäusler and Harré argue that first-person expressions mark both location in space and time as well as responsibility and social status.[79] This can happen through fine gradations of expressing certainty or doubt (compare 'I heard her say it!' and 'I think she said it') or through the use of different pronouns, depending on the social position one is speaking from: Japanese has a complex system of first-person pronouns for different levels of respect and formality; and the Royal 'We' can only properly be used by Her Majesty the Queen.[80]

Relevant for my purposes is the claim that first-person indexicals always do the double work: they mark the spatio-temporal location of the speaker *and* their position within a social infrastructure of proper language use.[81] Learning to use these indexicals properly is to learn how to be a person among other persons. 'The sense of self is not to be denied but for us it is a sense that each of us has of being located in certain ways relative to an environment of beings similar to ourselves.'[82] In these environments, we are inescapably both human animals and moral, political and social agents; and when children acquire the use of pronouns, they, too, learn how to be both an animal and an agent. There is nothing mysterious, however, about the use of these pronouns – they do not need to refer to some mysterious further fact of personhood in order to do their work: all that is needed is the recognition of their proper use by other speakers. This is the basis on which Mühlhäusler and Harré claim: 'That a person is recognized as one and the same person in different situations and at different times, we would call the *fact* of that person's identity.'[83] This recognition is more than having a sense of self and more than expressing this sense through language. It is expressing a sense of self in a context in which others can understand what it means, *without* having access to its internal formulation. What language does in this context is to provide a social structure in which 'private' sensory data (my feeling that I am an enduring self) can be expressed in such a way that they actually become independent of actual sensory input.

This is a theme to which we will return in chapter three, when we discuss modern identity management as the effort to decontextualize processes of recognition and thereby make them less intimate but more accessible. But next, we will consider the narrative view of personal identity – and some objections – in more detail. In replying to these objections, I hope to further defend a recognition account of personal identity.

NOTES

1. My summary of the case is based on journalistic profiles of Kyle's story: Megan Matteucci, 'A Real Live Nobody', *Savannah Morning News*, 24 September 2007, accessed 1 April 2016, http://savannahnow.com/news/2007-09-24/real-live-nobody#; Neil Forsyth, 'Do You Know This Man?', *The Guardian*, 10 July 2010, accessed 1 April 2016, http://www.theguardian.com/lifeandstyle/2010/jul/10/man-with-no-memory-america; Nathan Brown, 'Benjaman Kyle: A Man in Search of His Identity', *Nuvo: Indy's Alternative Voice*, 1 March 2013, accessed 16 February 2017, http://www.nuvo.net/indianapolis/benjaman-kyle-a-man-in-search-of-his-identity/Content?oid=2540059; and most recently and most detailed: Matt Wolfe, 'The Last Unknown Man', *New Republic*, 21 November 2016, accessed 30 May 2017, https://newrepublic.com/article/138068/last-unknown-man.

2. Vinnie Politan, Kelly Krammes and Julie Wolfe, 'DNA Expert: Man without Identity Wants It That Way', *11Alive Atlanta*, 5 February 2015, accessed 16 February 2017, http://legacy.11alive.com/story/news/crime/2015/02/01/man-lives-for-decade-not-knowing-who-he-is/22583483/; see also Wolfe, 'The Last Unknown Man' and Forsyth, 'Do You Know This Man'?

3. Wikstrom has made the film freely accessible on the video platform *Vimeo*, accessed 16 February 2017, https://vimeo.com/34589969.

4. Wolfe, 'The Last Unknown Man'.

5. The *Facebook* post is no longer available, but it was detailed in Kent Justice, 'Benjaman Kyle Writes "Thank You" Post: Man Learns his True Identity after 11 Years, Thanks those who Helped Him', *News4Jax*, 16 September 2015, accessed 30 May 2017, http://www.news4jax.com/news/benjaman-kyle-writes-thank-you-post.

6. Stephen Hudak, 'No-man's Land: Amnesia Stole His Identity for 11 Years', *Orlando Sentinel*, 22 September 2015, accessed 1 April 2016, http://www.orlandosentinel.com/news/local/os-benjamin-kyle-amnesia-identified-20150921-story.html.

7. Wolfe, 'The Last Unknown Man'.

8. Wolfe, 'The Last Unknown Man'.

9. Politan, Krammes and Wolfe, 'DNA Expert: Man without Identity Wants It That Way'.

10. Wolfe, 'The Last Unknown Man'.

11. To apply one of the core phrases Hilde Lindemann uses in her excellent and thought-provoking book, *Holding and Letting Go: The Social Practice of Personal Identities* (Oxford: Oxford University Press 2014).

12. Michael Quante, *Person* (Berlin and New York: Walter de Gruyter, 2007), 11; translation mine.

13. David Hume, *Treatise of Human Nature*, ed. David F. Norton and Mary J. Norton (Oxford: Oxford University Press, 2000), sect. 1.4.6, 165.

14. Derek Parfit, *Reasons and Persons* (Oxford: Clarendon Press, 1984), ch. 12.

15. Parfit, *Reasons and Persons*, 283.

16. Parfit, *Reasons and Persons*, 281.

17. Ibid.

18. Roughly speaking, part of what I am trying to defend here is the Wittgensteinian view of identity that Parfit dismisses in *Reasons and Persons,* 273. We will return to this Wittgensteinian view in the discussion of personal pronouns in section 1.6.

19. I am taking the notion of making people (and their social relations) legible from James C. Scott's study, *Seeing Like a State: How Certain Schemes to Improve the Human Condition Have Failed* (New Haven: Yale University Press, 1998); in particular from chapter 2, 'Cities, People, and Language', in which Scott discusses various ways in which the modern centralized state pursued this legibility project. I will discuss Scott's study in more detail in chapter 3.

20. Forsyth, 'Do You Know This Man?'

21. It might seem that these groups have little or nothing in common. As will become clear, however, modern identity management tends to approach these different groups with more consistency that one might think, and often with more consistency than one would wish for.

22. See, for instance, Elia Zureik and Mark D. Salter, *Global Surveillance and Policing, Borders, Security, Identity*, (Cullompton: Willan Publishing, 2005); Paisley Currah and Tara Mulqueen, 'Securitizing Gender. Identity, Biometrics, and Transgender Bodies at the Airport', *Social Research* 78:2 (2011), 557–582; Katja Franko Aas and Mary Bosworth (eds.), *The Borders of Punishment: Migration, Citizenship, and Social Exclusion* (Oxford: Oxford University Press, 2013).

23. The crucial passages here are the transcendental apperception (B132–B139) and the third paralogism of pure reason (A362–A367) in the *Critique of Pure Reason*, trans. Norman Kemp Smith (Basingstoke and London: Macmillan, 1990 [translation first published 1929]). As is customary, the *Critique of Pure Reason* is cited according to the original pagination of the first ('A') and the second ('B') edition of 1781 and 1787, respectively.

24. Marya Schechtman, *The Constitution of Selves* (Ithaca: Cornell University Press, 1996) and *Staying Alive: Personal Identity, Practical Concerns and the Unity of a Life* (Oxford: Oxford University Press 2014); and Lindemann, *Holding and Letting Go.*

25. David Lewis, 'Survival and Identity', in his *Philosophical Papers*, vol. 1 (Oxford: Oxford University Press, 1983), 57.

26. Schechtman, *Staying Alive*, 116.
27. Parfit, *Reasons and Persons*, 267.
28. Lewis, 'Survival and Identity', 58; Parfit, *Reasons and Persons*, 206. Parfit's and Lewis' Relation R is a development of John Locke's memory criterion of identity.
29. Parfit, *Reasons and Persons*, 267–268.
30. Lewis, 'Survival and Identity', 61 and 67.
31. This is Parfit's conclusion, in any case. David Lewis, who also discusses such fission cases comes up with the rather clever solution that there are two people even before the original is replicated, and each replica is thus identical to one of these pre-fission persons ('Identity and Survival', 65); see also the *Star Trek* example I discuss in section 1.4.
32. Sydney Shoemaker calls it 'Locke's Memory Theory', 'Personal Identity: A Materialist Account', in *Metaphysics: The Big Questions*, eds. Peter van Inwagen and Dean W. Zimmerman (Malden, MA: Blackwell Publishing, 1998), 296–310. The aptness of this characterization is still a controversial topic among metaphysicians and historians of philosophy – but that is an issue which need not concern us here, since the focus is on the contemporary re-imagination of Locke's theory as a psychological criterion of personal identity.
33. Locke, *Essay*, sect. II.XXVII.9, 335.
34. Thomas Reid, *Essays on the Intellectual Powers of Man*, ed. Derek R. Brookes (University Park: Pennsylvania State University Press, 2002), sect. III.6, 276; see also Shoemaker, 'A Materialist Account', 302–303. The example that follows is an adaptation of Reid's example of the 'brave officer'.
35. Parfit, *Reasons and Persons*, 205.
36. Such a view has been defended by at least one contemporary philosopher, Richard Swinburne, in 'Personal Identity: The Dualist Theory', in *Metaphysics: The Big Questions*, eds. Peter van Inwagen and Dean W. Zimmerman (Malden, MA: Blackwell Publishing, 1998), 317–333.
37. Modern identity management has come up with solutions that might seem as if they treated the body as a substance: fingerprinting or DNA-analysis, for instance. But fingerprinting and DNA analysis do not treat the body as a substance; rather, they treat certain particularly persistent bodily features as good evidence of personal identity. We will return to this subject in chapter 3.
38. Instead, I might cherish the fact that there are now two persons who have the same history and the same ambitions and desires; confer, Parfit, *Reasons and Persons*, 264.
39. The steps of the argument can be traced as follows: step 1) at Parfit, *Reasons and Persons*, 201 and 209; step 2) at Parfit, *Reasons and Persons*, 262–263; step 3) at Parfit, *Reasons and Persons*, 267; and step 4) at Parfit, *Reasons and Persons*, 268.
40. Lewis, 'Survival and Identity', 65.
41. Matt Wolfe aptly describes this as a 'civic death' in 'The Last Unknown Man'.
42. Cf. Maren Behrensen, 'Identity as Convention: Biometric Passports and the Promise of Security', *Journal of Information, Communication and Ethics in Society* 12: 1 (2014), 50–51.
43. Mühlhäusler, Peter and Rom Harré. *Pronouns and People: The Linguistic Construction of Social and Personal Identity* (Oxford: Basil Blackwell, 1990).

44. Marya Schechtman, *Staying Alive*, 2.

45. There is, however, an emerging literature in medical ethics about the psychological impact of surgical intervention and medication, especially the alteration of brain physiology or brain chemistry. I will return to this issue in chapter 2.

46. Locke already insisted on this analytic division in his account of personal identity (*Essay*, sect. II.XXVII.15, 340): 'I know that in the ordinary way of speaking, the same Person, and the same Man, stand for one and the same thing. ... But yet when we will enquire, what makes the same *Spirit*, *Man*, or *Person*, we must fix the *Ideas* of *Spirit*, *Man*, or *Person*, in our Minds; and having resolved with our selves what we mean by them, it will not be hard to determine, in either of them, or the like, when it is the *same*, and when not'. For explicit contemporary examples of this analytical approach, see Michael Quante, *Person*, and 'The Social Nature of Personal Identity', *Journal of Consciousness Studies* 14: 5–6 (2007), 56–76.

47. Locke, *Essay*, sect. II.XXVII.26, 346–347.

48. Locke, *Essay*, sect. II.XXVII.3–8, 330–335.

49. Locke, *Essay*, sect. II.XXVII.8, 332.

50. Locke, *Essay*, sect. II.XXVII.13–15, 337–340.

51. Locke, *Essay*, sect. II.XXVII.19, 342.

52. Locke, *Essay*, sect. II.XXVII.22, 343–344. Locke meets potential concerns about this backtracking from his original position by suggesting that God would know the full truth of the matter and properly deal with such cases on Judgement Day.

53. Kant, *Critique of Pure Reason*, A51/B75. Kemp Smith uses 'intuition' to translate the German *Anschauung*, which is one of the most difficult terms to translate in Kant's work. Very roughly speaking, *Anschauung* refers to the raw sensory input provided by our cognitive apparatus.

54. Kant, *Critique of Pure Reason*, A116.

55. Kant, *Critique of Pure Reason*, B421–422.

56. Kant, *Critique of Pure Reason*, A546/B574.

57. This 'knowledge' is not knowledge is the sense of predictive, empirical knowledge – for instance, knowledge to the effect that I can be certain that I will follow my moral compass in all possible circumstances. Rather, it is knowledge in the form of grasping an authority higher than one's own personal circumstances.

58. Christine Korsgaard, *Self-Constitution: Agency, Identity, and Integrity* (Oxford: Oxford University Press 2009), 18.

59. Korsgaard, *Self-Constitution*, 24.

60. Korsgaard, ibid.

61. Rae Langton, 'Duty and Desolation', *Philosophy* 67 (1992), 487.

62. Eric Olson, *What Are We?* (Oxford: Oxford University Press, 2007), 44.

63. Olson, *What Are We?*, 24.

64. Olson, *What Are We?*, 28.

65. See note 46.

66. Quante, 'The Social Nature of Personal Identity', 59–63.

67. Quante, 'The Social Nature of Personal Identity', 62.

68. Quante, 'The Social Nature of Personal Identity', 63. I will argue the opposite and suggest that such persistence conditions *must* be grounded in social practices and linguistic conventions, if we are to formulate them at all.

69. Quante, 'The Social Nature of Personal Identity', 65.

70. Ibid.

71. Moreover, there are reports of dementia patients who can be dragged out of their catatonia by playing music to them that they might remember from when they were young, or by creating an environment around them that reminds them of their youth. The Netherlands has a dementia village, Hogeweyk, that attempts to do just that, see its self-presentation at http://hogeweyk.dementiavillage.com/en/.

72. Quante, 'The Social Nature of Personal Identity', 69.

73. Schechtman, Staying Alive, 116–117.

74. Peter Mühlhäusler and Rom Harré, *Pronouns and People: The Linguistic Construction of Social and Personal Identity*, Oxford: Basil Blackwell 1990.

75. Peter Strawson, *Individuals: An Essay in Descriptive Metaphysics*, digital reprint (London and New York: Routledge, 2011), ch. 3, 'Persons'.

76. Mühlhäusler and Harré, *Pronouns and People*, 96, 115–116.

77. Mühlhäusler and Harré, *Pronouns and People*, 98–99.

78. Mühlhäusler and Harré, *Pronouns and People*, 92.

79. Ibid.

80. Mühlhäusler and Harré, *Pronouns and People*, 112–113.

81. Although the extent to which one or the other is emphasized varies among languages and linguistic situations.

82. Mühlhäusler and Harré, *Pronouns and People*, 87–88.

83. Mühlhäusler and Harré, *Pronouns and People*, 16.

Chapter 2

Narrativity and Normativity

As we have seen, the philosophical question about personal identity is in the first instance a question about what makes a person a person. Whatever the necessary conditions of personhood may be, the ability to verify their presence across time would seem to be a proper criterion for personal identity. On this view, personal identity becomes a mere problem of re-identification, that is, of reliably identifying the same person at different points in time.[1] From this view also spring the arguments I disputed in the previous chapter: First, Parfit's contention that identity does not matter and we should worry only about the continuity of mental life, in whichever form; second, the analytical attempts to separate different aspects of personhood, pick one and solve the puzzle of personal identity with it. I suggested that personhood is not a simple metaphysical fact, but a set of social practices, and that a social infrastructure, within which claims about the existence of persons are recognized, is a necessary condition for personhood and a sufficient condition for personal identity.[2] Whatever else – if anything – *might* be necessary for personhood (being a human animal, being conscious, being able to remember one's past and make plans for the future, being capable of moral deliberation) an infrastructure of different practices in which we treat each other as persons is required. These practices can range from the very intimate (expressing intense affection, comforting a loved one) to the personal but not intimate (holding a carpenter responsible for now showing up on the day they promised) to interaction between relative strangers (applying for a new identity card at the local registry office). So where there are persons, we should expect to find such practices; or without a social infrastructure, there are no persons. Where there is a social infrastructure that recognizes persons and holds them in their personhood, this infrastructure will avail create criteria for the recognition of individual persons, thus establishing personal identities across time. This view is different from the sceptical and analytical views we have encountered, since those views suggest that criteria for re-identification must be grounded in personal identity – and not the other way around.

I realize that the recognition view I defend here seems to lend itself to some rather strange conclusions: a hermit might not count as a person, but a spoiled family pet could be one. A provisional answer to such concerns touches upon three points:

1) A hermit, provided that they were properly socialized and enculturated, could return to his or her social existence at any point. Their personhood is on stand-by, but it has not been extinguished.
2) We have evidence that a lack of or deficiencies in the social infrastructure that supports practices of recognition hamper the development of attributes that are commonly associated with full personhood, such as the ability to learn to speak and write and to grasp and follow complex rules.[3] This observation is quite obviously circular – 'recognition presupposes recognition' – but not viciously so. Rather, it is a virtuous circle: if we can agree that recognition is a value and that the category of personhood incorporates this value, then we should support practices that foster recognition.
3) As for the case of potential non-human persons, we will have to look closely at *normative* reasons for inclusion or exclusion. Just as we might find reasons why we *ought to* recognize some human beings as persons although they are not yet or no longer rational and cannot yet or no longer fully reciprocate our practices of recognition, we might find reasons – now or in the future – why we ought to also regard some animals or artificial intelligences in this way.

We will return to these issues further, when discussing the risk that the recognition view can become so narrow – and so morally perverted – as to allow the mistreatment of human beings who deserve to be treated as persons.

2.1 IDENTITY AS SOCIAL REALITY

I have suggested that the recognition view is supported by the interpersonal and administrative practices of naming and identification that structure our lives. But this claim could be dismissed as circular, or it might be argued that practical concerns about identification are easily resolved by entertaining a pragmatic perspective on the limitations of both identity records and self-narrated accounts. That is to say, one might adopt the view that identity documentation can give only an incomplete picture of reality and is vulnerable to fraud. One might then suppose that whatever the physical or mental reality of personal identity is, identity documents can never fully capture it. This would explain both why there is epistemic and moral uncertainty around identity and how this uncertainty could, in principle, be minimized. However, such a view presupposes intrinsic criteria for identity, that is, physical or mental facts that can act as independent 'tie-breakers' when the patterns of social recognition fail to provide clear answers. Yet if there are no such independent facts, we seem to be left in the position that personal identity is a *mere* construction. And if personal identity is a construction, then the recognition view appears circular: personal identity exists and it matters, because people generally believe that it does. In what follows, I hope to take the edge off this potential objection to the recognition view by arguing for a third option: allowing that in some – but not necessarily all – cases independent evidence can and should have an impact on practices of recognition, while accepting both intimate and administrative narratives as a normative, rather than purely descriptive or epistemic framework of personhood. Let me start by offering a brief analogy to show how this might work.

Within the philosophy of biology, there is an ongoing debate about the ontology of sex and gender, that is, about the question of what sex and gender actually are. This debate has epistemic and practical import, since it concerns the various norms and practices by which we classify people (and animals) according to their perceived sex or gender. Consider the ongoing debate about sex 'verification' policies in professional sports.[4] Two equally straightforward – and in my view, equally naïve – positions mark the philosophical extremes one can adopt. One extreme is the naïve realist position that sex consists in a number of biological facts about chromosomes, gonads and hormones, and that these facts strictly determine the boundaries of socially available gender roles. In professional sports, current instantiations of this view are the 'hyperandrogenism' policies of the International Association of Athletics Federations (IAAF) and the International Olympic Committee (IOC), which ban women athletes with elevated levels of testosterone from competing in women's competitions, or regulations that force trans athletes to compete as the gender they were assigned at birth.[5] The other extreme is the naïve constructivist position that gender is merely a social convention and as such can be entirely decoupled from biological facts. In professional sports, it *would* be an instantiation of this view if governing sports bodies allowed athletes to pick their category based on self-identification alone.[6] Both positions have obvious philosophical problems, and both ultimately fail on account of the fact that even when gender is marked as 'social' and sex as 'biological', this does not imply that gender role, gender identity and sex can easily be decoupled from one another. Both extreme positions subscribe to a false dichotomy, namely that sex and gender must *either* be provable biological fact *or* fictitious social construction. But why not view sex and gender as a system of social organization bounded by biological elements?[7] The content of the categories of sex and gender and their enduring social importance can be best explained by pointing to their *function*. This functional explanation would give an account of the social meaning of gender roles: for instance, their continuing relevance for flirting and mating, for the division of domestic labour and care work and for the public perception of different kinds of personal qualities (strength, weakness, emotionality, rationality). Sex and gender are not simply individual constructions that can be chosen or dismissed on a whim. Rather, they are normative categories that maintain a social reality:[8] in our case, the reality of societies that make the gender dichotomy a central point of reference in many areas of social life. In this regard, sex and gender are *real as social conventions* that impose a normative order on our lives while appealing to the supposedly independent and objective authority of biological parameters.

Similar considerations can be applied to the concept of personal identity: we could agree with Hume or Parfit that there is no good philosophical, psychological or biological evidence for the existence of a unified, enduring self. But this does not compel us to ignore the social reality of the concept and the great variety of functions it serves: in interpersonal relationships, in art or in law. If we can accept that these social realities are no less real than biological or physical realities, then we have leverage to argue for the relevance and the reality of personal identity.

2.2 WHY NARRATIVE?

Narrative accounts of self and personhood have long been an object of psychological interest,[9] but in recent decades, they also experienced a revival in Anglophone philosophy. This revival came about from two different directions—metaphysical and ethical. While the metaphysical revival is directed primarily against Parfit-style 'no self' or 'identity does not matter' views, the ethical view is directed primarily against sociologically inspired and postmodernist 'many identities' or 'no unity' views. While the metaphysicians were concerned that their contemporaries had manoeuvred themselves into a philosophical corner from which they could no longer explain what it was they were talking about when they talked about persons, the ethicists were concerned that both modern and postmodern accounts of the self had left us with a splintered concept of personhood and moral agency that was in need of repair. It is no surprise that two of the most prominent philosophers in the 'ethical' camp were also accomplished historians of philosophy who made their case for narrativity and for a reconsideration of the postmodern self on the basis of scholarship deeply rooted in the history of Western philosophy:

Charles Taylor (in his monumental work, *Sources of the Self*) and Alasdair MacIntyre (in *After Virtue*).[10]

MacIntyre's target is the 'self separated from its roles' and the way 'in which modernity partitions each human life into a variety of segments, each with its own norms and roles for behaviour'.[11] He finds the sources of this splintered self in Erving Goffman's sociological theory of the modern American character[12] and in Sartre's existentialism with its exhortation to transcend social convention and remake oneself.[13] For Sartre, this radical constructionism represented the only way to be free and to be moral in modern society. For MacIntyre, it was a symptom of its sickness. He views both Goffman's and Sartre's visions of the self as fundamentally inauthentic: they lack unity and a true kernel of selfhood; a kernel from which the virtues can emerge. This is also MacIntyre's main ethical concern: the splintered self lacks a moral compass. Similarly, Charles Taylor is concerned with the unbounded self, one that lacks orientation in terms of stable 'horizons' of meaning, since those horizons (religious rites, local codes of conduct) have been wiped away by modernity[14] and replaced with ethical frameworks (Kantianism, utilitarianism) that lack depth. Correspondingly, he defines identity as follows:

> To know who I am is a species of knowing where I stand. My identity is defined by the commitments and identification which provide the frame or horizon within which I can try to determine from case to case what is good, or valuable, or what ought to be done, or what I endorse or oppose. In other words, it is the horizon within which I am capable of taking a stand.[15]

In the 'metaphysical camp' of the narrativists, what we find first and foremost is disappointment with the analytic tradition of thinking about personal identity, culminating in Parfit's *Reasons and Persons*. Perhaps the 'founding document' of this camp is Marya Schechtman's dissertation, published under the title *The Constitution of Selves* in 1996. Schechtman sets up her own argument by accusing the analytic metaphysicians of having asked the wrong question: instead of asking about *re-identification*, as they did, they should have asked about the *characterization* of individuals. She contends that to define identity in terms of re-identification

> is incoherent. The goal of offering a reidentification criterion is fundamentally at odds with the goal of defining personal identity in terms of psychological continuity, because psychological continuity as we ordinarily conceive of it has a logical form much different from that of an identity relation.[16]

Schechtman agrees with Parfit that re-identification theories of personal identity all run into the same problem: insofar, as they have to provide physical, psychological or mixed criteria for the identification of two individuals at two different points in time, they open the door for the branch-line cases we discussed in the previous chapter. Parfit concludes from this that identity is unimportant. Schechtman argues that this conclusion is much too hasty, because not all plausible theories of personal identity are re-identification theories. She calls her own alternative a 'characterization theory of personal identity', in which it is central to 'ask what it means to say that a particular characteristic is that of a given person'.[17]

This way of putting the question makes room for identity as narrative; for narratives can be used, among other things, to suggest whether someone is truly like *this* or like *that* and whether there are aspects of their personality that are more characteristic of them as an enduring person than others. Schechtman's concern with the characterization question can be linked back to practical concerns, for she argues that her account of narrative identity can make better sense of the practical question of self-identity – particularly self-regard and moral responsibility – than its competitors.[18] Here, her account has clear parallels with MacIntyre's worry about splintered modern selves; both believe that only an account of self and personal identity that is rooted in some sort of unifying narrative can help us make sense of our actions, desires and memories. MacIntyre makes this point by looking at the different ways in which one could answer the question, 'What are you doing?'[19] That I am sitting in my office on a Sunday afternoon, typing out sentences on my work computer can be made intelligible in different ways, and these different ways evoke different narratives. I could say: 'I was bored, and that's why I went to work for a bit.' Or I could say: 'I need to work on this book in order to get ahead in my job.' Or perhaps: 'Finishing this book is a deeply important personal project for me; I need to show myself that I can conclude a project like this.' Each of these answers evokes a different kind if narrative about me as a person; each of these makes sense only in relation to viewing me as a specific kind of character.

In recent years, narrative philosophy of identity has taken an even clearer turn towards social embeddedness. Schechtman, for instance, has revised her own account in her most recent monograph, *Staying Alive*, from a theory that emphasized self-narrative to a 'Person Life View'[20] that emphasizes the importance of the social environment in which these narratives take root. This strand of narrative analysis is of particular interest to me here, since my goal is to relate theories of personal identity to administrative and legal action, that is, to a previously overlooked aspect of the social environment in which person-lives are formed. Perhaps the most impassioned formulation of a social theory of narrative identity to date is Hilde Lindemann's, in her *Holding and Letting Go*. She considers the construction of identity narratives as 'identity work',[21] as a project in which people engage together by holding each other in their respective identities. It should be obvious why her view appeals to me, given what I have said about the social status of identity in the previous chapter. While Lindemann's concern is first and foremost with the construction of identities in intimate contexts – in families, between close friends, between caretakers and the people they care for – I believe that her central ideas can be transposed onto official identities and the state's work in creating and maintaining them. Consequently, I am going to suggest that even states and their agents can 'hold' people in their identities and 'let them go' and that moral conflicts in modern identity management typically occur when such 'holding' and 'letting go' is done stupidly, ineffectively or for the wrong reasons.

However, my main concern in the remainder of this chapter will be to deal with some of the strongest practical and philosophical objections to the narrative view. Galen Strawson, one of the sharpest critics of the narrative view of personal identity, has grouped these objections into two categories: those against the *psychological narrativity thesis* and those against the *ethical narrativity thesis*.[22] In addition to these, I will discuss some epistemic concerns with the narrative view, which relate closely to issues of identity management. In the final section, I will turn to the important question of whether a recognition view of personhood and identity would not open the door for individuals and regimes who want to deny personhood to those who deserve it.

2.3 THE PSYCHOLOGICAL NARRATIVITY THESIS

Strawson's view of the main moral risk of the narrative account can be reconstructed in direct opposition to ethical narrativists like MacIntyre. For MacIntyre, it is the non-narrative form that is inauthentic, for it lacks unity. For Strawson, it is narrativity itself that leads into inauthenticity. If someone were to tell themselves their own life in the form of a story, they might eventually become so entangled in it that they live their life as if it were a story; and for Strawson, this means that they would live their lives inauthentically, removed from their true selves, in the grip of narrative laws that are not truly their own. He writes: 'I think that those who think in this way are motivated by a sense of their own importance or significance that is absent in other human beings.'[23] Strawson here runs together his psychological and ethical worry: not only is it not the case that everyone has a narrative character, but those who do are in danger of seeing their own live as a bigger story than it actually is – and they will miss the best moments, for they will fail to live in the present.

I think this worry can be countered by paying close attention to what it is, exactly, that the narrative view is suggesting. We could, of course, take the narrative account in such a way that it suggests that we all *ought to construct a single autobiographical narrative* about our lives.[24] This interpretation does indeed have the obvious moral dangers Strawson alludes to. An alternative understanding, however, would be to understand narrativity as *one* basic way of making sense of our lives and of the events in it. The narrative form itself can convey meaning and 'explanatory force' to these events.[25]

A brief return to Kant's philosophical ambitions might help elucidate the point. In the *Critique of Pure Reason*, Kant was concerned with the problem of how to explain the generation of knowledge from disparate and diverse experiences and impressions. His answer was also an answer to David Hume, who had grappled with the same problem and come to the conclusion that there must be 'connexions' between the impressions themselves that would leave an imprint on our minds: if we observed often enough that a certain action had a certain effect, we would form the judgement that there must be a causal connection between the events.[26] Kant was not satisfied with Hume's empiricism, for it avoided the question of how such an order could arise in the first place: and it seemed to him that Hume's empiricism was either circular or not explanatory.[27] His reply to Hume was to locate the origin of causality in our own minds: causality is one of the categories, that is, one of the conceptual tools that allows us to make sense of the world.

Kant and Hume had a similar, indirect dispute about the issue of personal identity. As we have seen, Hume dismissed personal identity as a figment of the imagination. From his empiricist standpoint, he judged that there was absolutely nothing constant in his mind that would amount to a perception of himself as an enduring being. All he could observe was an ever-changing stream of different impressions: 'It cannot, therefore, be from any of these impressions, or from any other, that the idea of self is deriv'd; and consequently, there is no such idea.'[28] Kant, in the Transcendental Deduction of the *Critique of Pure Reason*,[29] accused Hume – and other empiricists – of a category mistake: he expected the self to be something that could be perceived, something that would have the same kinds of properties as those of an external object we can observe. But this was a misguided expectation. Hume's introspection treated the self as the putative object of an observation of which it could only ever be the subject. Indeed, the fact that Hume could perceive an ever-changing stream of consciousness was indicative of a subject of experience that appropriated all these impressions as 'mine' and then went on to proclaim that there was no 'me' to be found. For Kant, the subject of experience, and with it the concept of personal identity, were merely necessary conditions of the possibility of experience but not possible objects of experience.

An analogous point can be made about narrativity. Galen Strawson could be taken as the David Hume of the contemporary debate about personal identity. He looks inside himself and at literary and philosophical accounts of selfhood (or lack thereof) and finds that narrativity appears to be more of a flavour of character than a universal trait of self-regard. He distinguishes between 'episodics', who experience their lives in bits and pieces, and 'diachronics', who experience their lives under a larger narrative unity.[30] But being an episodic, in Strawson's view, is not a moral or epistemic disadvantage or deficiency. It is simply another mode of experience. And at this point, Strawson can be accused of the same category mistake that Kant accuses Hume of making. He looks inside himself and proclaims that he cannot find any traces of this 'narrative unity' of which other philosophers speak. Therefore, he concludes, it cannot exist; or in any case, its existence is not universal and it is not a necessary condition of moral personhood. Strawson does not doubt that there are some among us who have a strong narrative conception of themselves; but he stresses that many people do not. Like him, they see themselves as a fragmented collection of 'person-pieces' and experiences. He points to artists and novelists who break with the tradition of narrativity and do not tell stories but juxtapose literary fragments or write about themselves in a radically honest, unstoried way.[31] I do not doubt that the phenomenological experience of episodics or 'non-narratives' is real, and I do not dispute that it can be a powerful artistic tool or that it can serve as a stoic remedy against worrying too much about yourself. Yet it appears to me that Strawson's argument against the psychological thesis of narrativity suffers from the same problem as Hume's empiricist account of cognition; for the psychological thesis need not be taken as something that can or should be validated or falsified by introspection. Rather, it could be taken as a mode or form of the social cognition of persons, of which introspection is at best a part. The introspective claim that some people are not storytellers works against psychological generalizations such as: 'Human beings are natural storytellers.'[32] It does not affect the different claim that large parts of our social lives are organized in narrative terms. I might not have a tendency to put my own experiences in narrative form, and I might not enjoy telling stories about myself in front of others. This personal preference does not affect larger social tendencies that impose the narrative form on people – such as the self-promotion we have come to expect from political candidates or sports stars. Let us consider this social dimension of narrativity in relation to the two critical views that emerge from Stawson's anti-narrativist account: the 'no narratives' view and the 'many narratives' view. Both imply that narrativism is false, because there are no unifying narratives that structure our lives.

As I said, it might well be the case that human beings have different dispositions, some may consider themselves from the perspective of a storyteller, others might not, or they might do so at some times, but not at others. From this subjective perspective, it is impossible to argue with Strawson. But he overlooks a crucial point: the narratives that matter for the narrativists interested in social structures are rarely purely introspective. Like Hume, Strawson locks out his social environment – friends and colleagues who might have stories *about him* – to make his point. And like Hume, who famously named 'a game of back-gammon, [conversation and merriment] with friends'[33] as a remedy for his sceptical despair, Strawson might have wanted to look outwards before dismissing the narrative account. An 'identity-constituting narrative is not just a story you have about yourself but also the stories others tell about you', Schechtman writes.[34] For instance, stories I tell about my friends and the way I present them before others might affect the way these others treat my friends, which, in turn, might affect the way my friends view themselves. In this context, we might think of the practice of writing references, which quite clearly has an impact on how people present themselves as professionals.

For an account of narrativity that is insulated against Strawson's criticism from introspection, since it is explicitly not subject centred – but yet seeks to capture our most intimate relationships – we can look to Hilde Lindemann. For Lindemann, narrativity is 'identity work'. This is not work we do alone – nor work we can simply refuse to do – but something that we do with each other and something that we may sometimes be required to engage in. Personal identities, Lindemann says,

> are narratively constituted. They consist of tissues of stories and fragments of stories, generated from both first- and third-person perspectives, that cluster around what we take to be our own or others' most important acts, experiences, characteristics, roles, relationships, and commitments. . . . They are . . . narrative understandings formed out of the interaction between one's self-concept and others' sense of us.[35]

This mutuality and flexibility makes personal identities 'sites of contestation'.[36] But it also makes the narrative account at least partly independent of Strawson's classification of persons into narrative and non-narrative types. In Lindemann's account, as well as in Schechtman's revised account, narrativity is a social structure, not a subjective flavour of character or a personal perspective.[37] It is the means by which, for instance, families keep their memories or communities keep their traditions; and as such, it does not depend on what one person or as an individual can or cannot remember, or on what they are willing or unwilling to perform. This also takes care of another objection that could be levelled against the narrative view, namely that it is circular: 'If one must be a person in order to produce a self-narrative, then it is incoherent to suppose that being a person depends on already having produced a self-narrative.'[38] If 'having a narrative' means being embedded in a 'complex, normative, symbolically mediated organization we find in human societies',[39] then one can have a narrative even without being able to produce it oneself – something which would apply, for instance, to young children or people with dementia.[40] The point can be rephrased as follows: Strawson's psychological argument misses the relevant 'sites of contestation'. His argument suggests that the narrative account can be and should be rejected on empirical grounds, namely that it does not capture the lived reality of many people. I suggest that the relevant site of contestation is not empirical, but normative: if there are social structures that impose the narrative form on people, then questions of power and autonomy are crucial. If narrativity is a normative framework, then rather than asking whether people experience themselves as 'storytellers', we need to ask how that normative framework affects their abilities to define and assert themselves.

As already indicated, the account I develop here suggests that this narrative structure informs the administration of identities in public life and not just our private relations. Take as one example one's curriculum vitae (CV). Strawson is coy about having a poor memory and not being keen on telling stories about himself. But as an established professor of philosophy, there had to be instances in his life where he had to resort to narrative form: job applications and job interviews. CVs and cover letters are narrative form purified and stripped down to their bare minimum, and both are regarded as absolutely essential on the labour market. And even the most stalwart episodic types among us will have availed themselves of this form at some point – and thought hard about how to react to prompters like, 'So, tell us a bit about yourself and your motivation to apply for this job' in an interview. The CV example shows that whether or not narrativity exists and whether it is important for personal identity is not something that can be decided by introspection alone. These questions must be decided by looking at the social conditions that can force us to be a 'storyteller' – and even a narrativity sceptic can be forced to be one, quite independently of whether they are an episodic or a diachronic.

The example of the CV, however, points to another difficulty: that of competing narratives. When we apply for a job, we do, of course, try to present ourselves in the best possible light. We try to gloss over gaps in our employment histories, reinterpret failures as opportunities and focus on useful skills rather than personal interests. In extreme cases, the process of putting together an application perhaps can feel as if we are two different persons: one public and flawless; the other private and flawed. Similar observations can no doubt be made about persons who live a variety of different and disconnected private lives, or those who feel that their mood and personality depend heavily on their company and circumstances. If we take a strong 'many narratives' position – if we hold that persons are fundamentally not one but many narratives – do we get a strong argument against the narrative view as such?

Erving Goffman popularized the idea that we play many roles in our daily lives: at work, at home, in school, among friends. He assumes that 'when an individual appears before others he will have many motives for trying to control the impression they receive of the situation'; and his scholarship 'is concerned with some of the common techniques that persons employ to sustain such impressions'.[41] Some of these roles are clearly incompatible, or at least we should consider them to be: 'abusive parent' and 'child-care specialist', for instance. And sometimes, the projection of a role goes embarrassingly wrong: I remember, for instance, when I visited the HR department of one of the colleges where I taught after my graduation and was asked whether I was 'the new sports coach' – because I was wearing a Red Sox cap. With the emergence of social media, managing different social roles and the different expectations tied to them has become an even greater challenge for many people; political careers, for instance, can be upended by an embarrassing photo or an ill-considered tweet. Lawyers and computer ethicists have even argued for a right to be forgotten, since the 'apparently perfect (digital) memory may ultimately make a person lose his fundamental capacity to live and act in the present because the person is constantly persecuted and hampered by their frozen past'.[42] Insofar as the narrative view presupposes that a person's narrative has some underlying unity, the variety of professional and personal roles we fill over the course of our lives appears to threaten that unity. But how much of a threat is this, really?

While phenomenologically speaking, it appears correct to say that most people – at least in Western societies – draw a rather sharp line between public and private aspects of their personality, it would be an exaggeration to conclude from this that they are literally all living separate lives at work and home. Consider the typical process of 'getting to know someone': you might be surprised to learn that someone you know from work has a colourful private personality, but you need not feel deceived. Where the feeling of deception is warranted, the person would already have given the impression that they are something they are not, which is importantly different from discovering an aspect of their personality you simply did not know about before.[43] For instance, if you have given the impression that you are a warm and caring person, but then I catch you hurling abuse and threats at beggars, I might rightfully feel deceived. If I have taken you for a quiet and withdrawn person, but then I learn that you really enjoy karaoke, I would be surprised but not feel deceived. The relevant difference here is between selectively revealing information about you, depending on the context you are in and keeping information secret, because you know it would undermine the image you want to project in a given context. While the difference between the two might sometimes be blurry, it can in principle serve to meet the 'many narratives' objection: as long as there is no sense that different aspects of a personality undermine each other, or that a particular role we play is not simply adapted to a given context but designed to deceive, the objection does not stick. In positive terms: the unity of a personal narrative can be maintained throughout different professional and private roles we play, as long as these roles have some underlying coherence. Moreover, conflicting and contradictory narratives always bear the potential for exposure. A secret life hidden from one's family or blatant lies on one's CV are serious risks, and upon discovery, they will exact a social and moral price. They do not become less of a lie or less of a secret life just because they are embedded in narrative form – for in such cases, we have facts which can undercut the entire narrative.

2.4 FORENSIC AND ADMINISTRATIVE NARRATIVES

I have suggested that modern identity management can be understood as a set of narrative technologies. In what follows, I shall explain what I mean by that and how this fits with my contention that narrativism can be defended against the relativist contention that 'anything goes'. The claim that identity management is narrative in form might seem rather odd; after all, it is about determining the truth and falsity of identity claims. These verifications occur at particular points in time, and they would thus seem to be isolated events, not some parts of a larger narrative. Here it is instructive to once again consider the example of identity theft and fraud: the fraudster's challenge is *not* to pass an isolated identity check here or there; their challenge is to have a convincing story about themselves, a story that will be believed at different times and in different places. And the detective's challenge is to uncover the fraudster and to put them into a position where their narrative falls apart. Of historical interest in this context is a collection of criminal cases from the United States and France, published in 1854 under the title *Cases of Personal Identity*.[44] Among articles reprinted from newspapers of that period, the volume also contains an extensive account of the case of Martin Guerre, a French peasant of the sixteenth century, who had disappeared from his village for eight years, then supposedly returned, and was later exposed as an impostor by the real Martin Guerre. This case, as well as the others assembled in the volume, depends heavily on the use of narrative for its solution: Martin Guerre's and the impostor's memory are probed for inconsistencies that could give them away; Guerre's wife and other family members are asked for their accounts; and in the end, the tearful testimony of Guerre's sister sways the judges' and the audience's opinion – and the impostor is convicted and executed.[45]

If we compare this story to modern forensic methods, we might be tempted to think that things have changed significantly: we have fingerprinting and DNA analysis; we have *objective* methods to convict criminals. However, it would be false to describe these changes as a simple shift from subjective to objective methods.[46] Testimony still plays a central role in court proceedings; and the methods of forensic science often fail to produce the sort of evidence that would be useful without testimony. The suspect's fingerprints might be at the scene of the crime, but how can a motive be established? Forensic evidence might also be misleading: DNA samples can be contaminated and fingerprints taken from crime scenes are hardly ever complete prints.

> Forensic fingerprint identification . . . ultimately . . . rests on the . . . ambitious premise that no two *partial* prints are alike, or that fragmentary areas of papillary ridge detail . . . can be matched to one and only one finger, to the exclusion of all other fingers in the world. Morever, the impressions are often blurred, smudged, overlaid upon on [*sic*] another, and distorted by foreign matter.[47]

Conversely, the core principles of forensic science are not exactly recent inventions: during Martin Guerre's trial in the sixteenth century, the judges tried to establish his identity by using 'biometric' criteria like the location of birthmarks on his body. The practices of modern forensics have a long history, and they are embedded in social practices that permit and sometimes encourage the narrative form – think of the prosecutor who constructs a story around fingerprint evidence to show that not only were the defendant's prints found at the scene but they also had a motive to kill the victim.

We can extend this observation to more mundane practices of identity verification. Each visa stamp in my passport, for instance, tells a part of the story of my seven years of legal residence in the United States; and each stamp solidifies my story – presenting myself as a former grad student and 'legal alien' – in the eyes of a border guard who meets me for the first time. It is no coincidence that border guards are trained not only to quickly glean all available information from a traveller's documents but also to spot signs of anxiety or overconfidence that might betray a lie. Each individual administrative act thus becomes part of a larger narrative: a birth certificate is not simply a record of a particular event at a particular time, it also lays the groundwork for all future legal identification; a passport is not simply an entry ticket to another country, it typically implies the existence of a trail of administrative records that were involved in its issuance, and it can quite obviously tell a travel history. Schechtman makes a similar point when she emphasizes that taking a specific attitude towards another human being *as a person* is, in many instances, an institutional practice:

> [It] means . . . that human infants are dressed in clothes and their births recorded; that human children are generally exposed to certain kinds of education; that all humans are subject to the laws of the land and can potentially be arrested and

brought to trial if there is reason to think that they have willfully violated them; that they are eligible qualify for social welfare programs; and so on.[48]

All of these institutional practices that serve to recognize persons in their personhood, in turn, depend on practices of identification – on the small administrative acts that contribute to the larger picture. But these practices are, of course, not flawless – the 'larger picture' might be misleading – and this is a concern to which we will return.

2.5 EPISTEMIC AND MORAL CONCERNS

One obvious and strong objection to the narrative view of personal identity is of an epistemic nature. If the concept of identity has a social purpose, then we need appropriate criteria for its use. For instance, if identity partly consists in the possession of identity documents, then we need appropriate criteria for the use and verification of such documents. If no such criteria can be established, then we seem to be left with the untenable situation that 'anything goes' in matters of identity. The problem also besets more 'intimate' accounts of narrative identity. Lindemann explores the fictional case of a friend and caretaker to an elderly professor who has expressed his desire for 'a natural death'.[49] The elderly professor suffers a heart attack with several complications, and the caretaker now finds himself in a position where he tries to urge the attending doctor to stop treatment for fear that his friend will end up in a state where he is permanently dependent on machines. The question Lindemann poses through this story is whether the friend is trying his best to hold the professor in his identity or he is attempting to sabotage a possible restructuring of the professor's own wishes in light of the doctor's attempts to keep him alive. Lindemann ascribes the following train of thought to the caretaker:

> His biggest fear was that when they waked Edmund [the elderly professor] the next morning, he would say yes and improve just enough to end up in a nursing home, with one complication after another until he finally died. I've got to stop that, he thought, but I can't see how. . . . Somehow, I've got to convince them to let him die tonight, before he has any chance to get better.[50]

The story does not easily lend itself to a clear judgement of whether the friend holds the elderly professor in his identity poorly or properly – and Lindemann refuses to give a straightforward answer. She describes the case as one where two equally intelligible narratives clash: that of an old but healthy man who expresses his wishes never to be dependent on life-support; and that of an old, very sick man who might want to cling on to what little life he has left, even if that means constant medical care.[51] These narratives even overlap in terms of what the relevant facts of the case are. There is a good chance that the only option for the old man's survival is constant care in a nursing home. For his friend, this possible reality is something that violates his identity narrative; for the doctors, it does not, since they suppose that 'people change their minds' when they actually become critically ill. This is a case, then, which cannot be resolved by an appeal to narrative: the friend and the doctor may well agree that, yes, the man signed an advance directive against life support, and yes, his deteriorating health might require precisely that – but they can still disagree as to how the patient's wishes are to be understood. Do we take the content of the directive as binding, or do we ask him now? Does it even make sense to ask what 'the patient's wishes' are, given that these wishes might change rather dramatically with the new situation?[52]

Similar ethical issues have surfaced in other areas of modern medicine, and they, too, are being discussed in terms of narrativity. Philosophers and doctors are currently debating potential ethical constraints on deep brain stimulation for patients with psychiatric and neurological diseases – a concern triggered by reports of Parkinson's patients who underwent drastic personality changes after treatment.[53] Likewise, medication for depression and anxiety is sometimes met with scepticism and hesitation – by patients and by ethicists – because it supposedly bypasses one's 'true' personality and is therefore inauthentic.[54] Some of this hesitation can be explained by the overprescription of these drugs in some countries, especially the United States ('Generation Prozac'), where they are often taken by people who do not need them. But the worry can be fleshed out in a different way, much closer to our concern here: patients struggling with clinical depression sometimes hesitate for a long time before they choose to take the medication they have been prescribed, for fear of what it might say about them if they medicate. A good friend who was diagnosed with severe depression described this conflict as follows: for months, she was convinced that she needed to overcome her depression on her own, by force of will and 'natural means' such as exercise, mindfulness and strict routines. Her narrative at the time did not allow her to consider the drug as a legitimate 'jumpstart' for this effort. In addition, she was concerned that the drug would affect her libido (a well-documented side effect in many anti-depressants), something which she also regarded as essential to her self-conception.[55] And, of course, there was the possibility that the drug might actually worsen the symptoms of her depression and increase her anxiety. After she decided to go on the medication and her depression got much better, she described these fears as misguided. What the drug had actually done was to bring back aspects of her personality that she had lost to her depression: the ability to enjoy music, art or the company of friends. And what seemed like giving in to a drug now became the chemical 'push' she needed to become emotionally stable and be able to tackle the underlying causes of the depression. So which narrative is correct? Some people with depression never get better on drugs; some experience improvement as well as changes in their personality which they regard as unpleasant or inauthentic; some experience improvement and say that it feels as if a dark cloud has been lifted from them. Since anti-depressants can have all these effects, worries that patients may have cannot be addressed simply by telling them that the drug will 'restore' their personality. It is more complicated than that.

In cases like these, the narrative account appears to leave us with an epistemic deadlock. We do not seem to be able to say which narrative matters more: the one of the hesitant patient or the patient who is glad that they took the medication; the narrative of the person who signed an advance directive, or the narrative of the person who is woken from their induced coma and decides that they do, in fact, want to continue 'living like this'. In these problem cases, the epistemic deadlock can, however, be resolved by turning to the moral values at stake:

> From the standpoint of the physician, there may be an obligation to respect the autonomous wish of a former competent patient. Yet this may come into conflict with professional duties to provide what is recognized as appropriate therapy to a patient who has succumbed to serious impairment.[56]

It is perfectly understandable that doctors refuse to think about narrativity and autonomy in such instances and insist to care only about the human animal: for the consequences of letting the human animals die are graver than a possible infringement on their patient's wishes.[57]

But while these cases may not lend themselves to showing how the narrative view can resolve these issues, they do show how we can make sense of the conflicts experienced by people who end up in these situations as patients or concerned friends or family members. Furthermore, these difficult cases should not be taken as indicative of *all* the circumstances in which narrative identity may play a role; for in many of them, epistemic conflicts can be resolved.

If I claim, for instance, that I have never visited the United States before, and my passport shows a visa for the United States and a number of entry and exit stamps, then a border guard would be quite right to discount my in-person narrative and usher me aside for further questioning. Or if I claim that I have never been sick in my life but my medical records say otherwise, then there would be good reason for, say, an insurance claims specialist to disregard my assurances. So we can at the very least formulate the following minimal requirement for narrative integrity: identity narratives must not contradict available independent evidence.[58] To formulate this requirement in a cautious way leaves room for differing interpretation of the same event – my medical records, for instance, might contain misdiagnoses – but it rules out the possibility that one person could claim that something has happened and the other that it has not, and with both being right because that 'something' fits the first person's narrative, but not the second person's. In other words: making the narrative account receptive to independent evidence opens up the possibility that some narrative can be proven wrong – or at least shown to be less plausible than their competitors – in light of evidence.

Of course, independent evidence does not often come in the shape of simple, indisputable, objective facts. The earlier fingerprint example shows this, as does Lindemann's case study or the complex understanding of sex and gender, which I discussed in the introduction to this chapter. Take as an example of this difficulty the ways in which narrative instantiations of childhood experiences may differ. Suppose that your parents see themselves as kind and loving people who always wanted the best for you and always supported you in your plans. You, however, see them as distant and disinterested people who never quite seemed to understand what it was that you wanted for yourself and what it is that you are doing now. A debate about these differing narratives could easily ruin a family holiday, even – or especially – if independent evidence is introduced: 'We paid for your studies because we trusted you to make the right decisions!' – 'Yeah, but you never read anything I wrote, and you never really listened when I told you about the books I was reading!' – and so on.

The problem here seems to be that the 'independent' evidence is not so independent after all; it has acquired a specific meaning in both your and your parents' narrative: 'money' for your parents might denote support, while for you it denotes alienation. Now we could claim that all supposedly independent evidence is embedded in such narratives: narratives of how our society functions, of how we do science, and of how we establish and refute certain claims in court. This observation might seem a fatal blow to the narrative account: if no evidence is truly independent, then how can we avoid the conclusion that narratives really are just arbitrary constructions, which appropriate evidence as needed? I will return to this issue in chapter four, when I discuss the question of how identity documents aim to establish knowledge of a person. In what follows, I want to emphasize one important aspect that distinguishes the hypothetical quarrel with your parents from narrative issues as they occur in law or administration. The latter are embedded in larger institutions that offer checks and balances on individual – and potentially misleading – narratives.

2.6 EXPOSING THE FRAUDSTERS

These checks and balances do not make institutions immune against any and all mistakes – we will consider that point in the following chapters – but they do constitute safeguards against fraud and arbitrariness. As a social and legal institution, identity documents work (most of the time) because there are regulations that stipulate under which conditions and with which specifications these documents are to be issued to which persons. These regulations are sometimes shoddily drafted and sometimes applied carelessly or with ill intent, but as a general rule, they ensure that not just *any* narrative can claim epistemic validity when it comes to official recognition. It is instructive to consider what can happen when these safeguards are not used or when regulations are followed in a haphazard way.

A recent example is the case of Paolo Macchiarini, an Italian surgeon, who wildly exaggerated his accomplishments and his academic status and invented positions he had never held in order to boost his reputation as one of the world's leading surgeons. Macchiarini was hired by Karolinska Institute (KI) and the Karolinska University Hospital, Sweden's leading research hospital, in 2010. While at the University Hospital, he conducted at least three trachea transplants with synthetic tissue in 2011 and 2012. These procedures were highly experimental and led to serious complications, which eventually resulted in the death of all the patients. Macchiarini's reckless surgical projects were not stopped by any ethics review, and he was initially praised for advancing the science of transplanting synthetic tissue. In reality, however, he was conducting an unsanctioned and lethal human trial. Despite concerns about his conduct as a researcher and surgeon, his contract with KI was extended in 2013 and 2015 without any proper review of his activities.[59] When the Macchiarini case eventually became the subject of an official investigation and the focus of a national crisis of higher education in Sweden, it was found that KI had ignored reports about Macchiarini's dishonest and boastful behaviour and the embellishments on his CV even before he was hired in 2010, shortly after he had been prevented from receiving a professorship in Italy for just these reasons. The external report on the case's handling by KI suggests that the management may have been blinded by their desire to hire a researcher of seemingly international stature.

As it turns out, Macchiarini was not just an academic conman but also a notorious liar in his private life. An article in *Vanity Fair*[60] details the lies he told a news producer who had fallen in love with him; perhaps the most blatant one of which was that he would get Pope Francis to officiate their marriage ceremony because he was the pontiff's personal physician – the marriage never happened, and at the Vatican, no one knew who Macchiarini was.

We could take the Macchiarini case and cases of conmen like him as damning evidence against the viability of the narrative view of personal identity. Macchiarini told stories about himself that were, to a large extent, pure fiction; and what was true in them, he exaggerated. It was because of his charm and his victims' personal motives that the latter believed him. This, in any case, seems true of KI's management and of his former fiancée: the former hoped to gain a world-class surgeon in an increasingly competitive environment for institutions of higher learning; the latter was taken by Macchiarini's presentation of himself as a perfect gentleman. If so, then according to the view that I have been defending so far, it would seem that whatever Macchiarini chose to tell about himself constituted his real identity – until he was exposed and shamed for it. There is no difference between the story and the man; his reality is his deception, and his deception is his reality.

Now, Erving Goffman distinguishes between persons who come to believe in the roles they are playing and 'cynics' who never get to that point.[61] The former might be more likely of pathological liars like Macchiarini – that is, they come to believe in their own lies – but this does not mean that we have to accept their mendacious narratives as the last or the most important word on who they are. And even where deception is self-deception, it can be exposed and remedied.[62] One can understand the discrepancy between Macchiarini's aggrandizing self-presentation and the cautionary tales about his actual achievements and failures as competing narratives. But it can nevertheless be argued that the critical reports about his person are more trustworthy and that we do not merely have an issue of Macchiarini's word against that of his detractors. The investigation into KI's handling of his case found that the committee that appointed him disregarded negative reports about his actual qualifications and previous instances of boasting and fraud. Hence, the committee violated established procedure for the selection of candidates for an academic position. They disregarded basic epistemic safeguards – and it must be emphasized that such safeguards are in place for *moral* reasons: namely, to protect patients (and the scholarly community) from people like Macchiarini.

We could perhaps make a similar assessment of the woman who fell for his charm: had she stopped to consider whether what he told her *could* even be true – how likely is it *really* that even the most dashing surgeon has a personal relationship with the Pope, such that the Pope will officiate at his wedding? – then she could have avoided bitter disappointment and heartbreak. David Velleman warns that narrative explanation can sway emotionally without any real evidence, and people like Macchiarini certainly use this emotional sway for their own ends. However, Velleman also insists that the emotional impact 'of narrative history is not itself an illusion or projection – not, at least, unless all emotion involves an illusion or projection of a significance that events do not really have'.[63] Macchiarini's fiancée might have had friends who would have warned her, or as a journalist, she might have been aware of how conmen operate. Perhaps drawing the right connections could have prevented her from falling for his lies.

The social space in which narratives play out is shaped by emotions and desires. But it is also shaped by social and legal norms, which can function as a check on those emotions – and which are designed to protect people from disappointment and harm. The purpose of such norms is primarily normative, not epistemic. Among them, for instance, are the criteria for the selection of a candidate for an academic position – as well as social understandings regarding what you can and should expect in terms of honesty from a partner (although the latter will of course be much less rigorous than the former). In this web of norms, no single identity narrative makes an identity. No one's isolated claim to be this or that person, to have done this or that, or to belong to this or that group makes that claim true. Such claims are always being lodged within a system of established norms – and most importantly, they are launched and challenged as moral claims and not as purely epistemic claims.

Take as an example the ongoing controversies about the legal recognition of trans and genderqueer identities. It is sometimes suggested by critics that letting persons use the public toilets that align with their lived gender, or opening women's competitions in professional sports to intersex athletes would open the door to 'men posing as women'.[64] The assumption behind these complaints is that allowing trans and genderqueer persons to occupy certain spaces would set a dangerous precedent for men with criminal or fraudulent intent. This can be understood in one of two ways: either it can be taken to mean that trans and genderqueer persons themselves (like our hypothetical male impostors) are 'fraudsters', a toxic trope which Talia Mae Bettcher has deconstructed carefully and poignantly;[65] or it can be taken to mean something like: 'If we allow this, then anyone can claim to be anything, and no one can prove them wrong.' It is both interesting and disturbing to observe how much sway the second interpretation seems to hold, since this sway often betrays a near-complete ignorance of the social structures within which the identity claims of trans persons are being lodged.

Transitioning is a social *process* that requires time, energy and often significant financial resources; it is never just an isolated claim. Where transitioning is socially and legally possible at all, it is likely to involve very difficult conversations with friends and family members and frustrating experiences with the authorities and health care providers, whom a trans person typically needs to enlist to support their case for a change of their legal sex (I will say more about this issue in chapter four). When a trans person, after or during the process of transitioning, wants to use the public toilet that fits their lived gender, this is nothing like a cisgender male trying to sneak into the women's toilet.

So the question we need to ask is not 'Are trans women really women?' but 'Under the conditions I just summarized, are there any compelling *moral* reasons to deny a trans person the use of the toilet that best represents their lived gender?' Indeed, those who represent trans persons as 'deceivers' and 'make-believers' are making moral claims as well, and so, the proper way of challenging them is to question whether such claims can withstand ethical scrutiny: Does the recognition of trans persons undermine important security interests? Are they, in turn, harmed if recognition is denied them? If we consider these questions – and answer 'no!' to the first one and 'yes!' to the second – we are no longer asking an epistemic or metaphysical question about sex and gender. We are forced to consider the discrimination and the violence trans women are exposed to where they are not recognized as women.

Similar considerations can be applied to professional sports. The risk of national and global humiliation for intersex athletes is so high – as the case of Caster Semenya has shown – that it is difficult to imagine that persons with a stereotypically male anatomy would deliberately pose as women to gain a competitive edge. The social structure within which one can claim that her 'sporting gender' is female is such that trying to cheat is nothing like being a man being told he should pose as a woman in athletics. There is an entire host of regulations and social incentives around the issue that would prevent this from happening.

Lastly, consider the fear that terrorists might pose as refugees in order to get easy access to their European targets; and conversely, that asylum-seekers might be 'anyone' if they cannot provide identity documents. Admittedly, this issue is not as easily dismissed as the first two. Asylum-seekers have committed (or planned to commit) acts of terror – for instance, the axe attack in a local train near Würzburg, Bavaria, in June 2016; or the truck attack on the Christmas market at the Breitscheidplatz in Berlin in December 2016; or the case of the *Bundeswehr* soldier who was arrested in April 2017, because he allegedly posed as a Syrian refugee – despite speaking only a few words of Arabic – in order to commit a false flag terror attack.[66] Furthermore, there are good reasons to believe that some refugees do indeed throw away their identity documents in order to pose as someone from another country with more chance of receiving asylum or another form of refugee protection – an Iraqi citizen, for instance, might want to pose as Syrian for this reason. Now does this mean that 'anything goes' in terms of what refugees say about themselves? Can they just make any claim about themselves and their history and rightly have it believed by authorities? The answer to these questions, at least in countries with a functioning administrative apparatus, is clearly no. While there are loopholes in every system, each one of these systems also has safeguards. In refugee interviews in Germany, officials are supposed to be trained to ask questions to determine the actual origin of an asylum-seeker – in order to obviate fraudulent claims about their origin. If the system has been struggling to cope with the number of asylum-seekers that reached Germany in 2015 and 2016 and if incompetent or poorly trained personnel were hired because of these struggles, this does not mean that the system could not be reformed accordingly. An extreme example of safeguards is the United States, where refugees accepted for resettlement must pass an arduous vetting process. Passing these checks with a fake identity is virtually impossible.[67]

What this means in general terms is that there is no such thing as an epistemic free-for-all in identity claims. Social and legal systems typically work in such a way as to account for the possibility that people might make entirely fake claim about themselves, and so sooner or later these people will hit a bureaucratic wall at which their stories can be discounted; just like a fraudster in social circles – like Macchiarini – runs the risk of having his wild claims exposed.

2.7 DEHUMANIZATION AND DEPERSONALIZATION

We have considered one general objection to the narrativist view, which held that narrativism would entail that *any* narrative I choose to tell about myself would become the truth simply in virtue of me telling it. With Marya Schechtman's reformed narrativist view, which holds that person-narratives must always be embedded in and checked against a social infrastructure of recognition,[68] we can counter this objection. But by tying the validity of person-narratives to social recognition, we open up another line of objection: what happens if the social infrastructure, instead of recognizing persons, refuses to grant them the social and legal status typically entailed by personhood? Schechtman discusses this under the heading of 'anomalous social position',[69] and notes that '[h]istory . . . is full of examples where one group of humans treats another group of humans as non-persons and prevents them from living a person life'.[70] This consideration might, for instance, be applied to refugees where they are treated as mere bodies or as a mere statistic and not recognized as individual persons. So if recognition is indeed essential for personhood and personal identity, as both my own view and Schechtman's Person Life View suggest, does this not imply that lack of recognition actually destroys personhood and personal identity; and if so, that human beings who are denied recognition as persons are *not actually* persons, no matter how much they themselves may insist on that status? If narrativism presupposes social recognition, and if such recognition can be withheld in manifestly harmful and morally objectionable ways, then how do narrativists escape the seemingly obvious conclusion that their view of personhood cannot maintain that the withholding of recognition is indeed immoral?

Schechtman counters this sort of objection by pointing out that the worst cases of dehumanization – genocide, slavery, the use of rape as a weapon of war – are the worst, precisely because they build on the recognition that the killed, enslaved or raped person is a *person* and then insist that nonetheless *anything* can be done to them. Drawing on Stanley Cavell's reflections on the matter, Schechtman points out that the slaveholders or the misogynists do not actually believe that slaves or women are not persons. Rather, they believe that they are *lesser kinds of persons*; for if they were non-persons, detailed legal regulations of slaves' lives or impassioned pleas against women's suffrage would be pointless.[71] What is at stake in the worst cases of dehumanizing treatment is not mere lack of recognition but a perverse recognition: The raping soldier knows that his victim is a person and that is why he rapes – because the rape breaks the person in front of him, and by extension, humiliates the group to which they belong. The online troll who advocates killing disabled people knows that disabled people are indeed treated as persons by most others – which is exactly what makes their trolling effective, because it enables them to get a rise out of a other people.

A similar logic of perverse recognition drives administrative efforts that marginalize and dehumanize entire groups. Purges and genocides require that their victims are recognized by the perpetrators and in their recognition distinguished from *other people like them*. Stalin's purges presupposed extensive record-keeping of individual citizens – records that marked them as 'untrustworthy' or 'bourgeois', thus set them up for their later deportation and destruction. The same is true – although with less deadly consequences – for the 'Communist scare' that gripped the United States in the 1950s: people were hauled in to testify before the House Un-American Activities Committee in order to prove that they were not sympathizing with or agitating for the Soviet Union. The Rwandan genocide of 1994 may not have been possible without the efforts of a Belgian colonial administration that classified the population of what was then part of the territory of Ruanda-Urundi as Hutu and Tutsi. And the registration and subsequent marginalization of Jews was a cornerstone of the Nazis' anti-semitic policies and formed the basis of the Jews' eventual deportation and industrial mass murder (to which we will return in chapter four). These measures do not mark their victims as non-persons; rather, they mark them as a different *kind* of person – and they are the most serious moral risk of contemporary identity management. Before we turn to this issue, however, the next chapter will explore the modern logic of identity management – including its potential benefits. This will set the change for a nuanced analysis of the aforementioned moral risks.

NOTES

1. Cf. Schechtman, *The Constitution of Selves*, 7–25. Schechtman identifies this focus on re-identification as a central flaw of psychological continuity theorists like Locke and Parfit.

2. Cf. Schechtman, *Staying Alive*, 114–118.

3. See, for instance, one of the first articles in psychology that investigated the importance of social networks for child development: Moncrieff M. Cochran and Jane Anthony Brassard, 'Child Development and Personal Social Networks', *Child Development* 50:3 (1979), 601–616.

4. Cf. Susan Cahn, 'Testing Sex, Attributing Gender: What Caster Semenya Means to Women's Sports', *Journal of Intercollegiate Sport* 4 (2011), 38–48; Katrina Karkazis et al., 'Out of Bounds? A Critique of the New Policies on Hyperandrogenism in Elite Female Athletes', *The American Journal of Bioethics* 12:7 (2012), 3–16; Maren Behrensen, 'In the Halfway House of Ill-Repute: Gender Verification under a Different Name, Still no Contribution to Fair Play', *Sport, Ethics, and Philosophy* 7:4 (2013): 450–466.

5. Such regulations recently became the focus of controversy when a Texas high school student – a trans boy – was forced to compete in the girls' class in the state championships and easily won, in part, because he had been on testosterone for a year and a half. The boy himself reportedly insists that he wants to compete against boys. See Camila Domonoske, '17-Year-Old Transgender Boy Wins Texas Girls' Wrestling Championship', NPR.org, 27 February 2017, accessed 30 March 2017, http://www.npr.org/sections/thetwo-way/2017/02/27/517491492/17-year-old-transgender-boy-wins-texas-girls-wrestling-championship.

6. Letting allegedly intersex athletes like Caster Semenya compete in the women's category is sometimes perceived to be on the same level as allowing men to claim that they are women in order to easily win. This perception is entirely false and misleading, since at least in professional sports on the international level, the participation of trans and intersex athletes is strictly regulated. I will return to the trope of the 'male impostor' when I discuss 'bathroom bills' that force some trans persons to use public toilets that do not correspond to their lived gender.

7. For a critical metaphysical account of the sex/gender distinction, see Mari Mikkola, 'Ontological Commitments, Sex, and Gender', in *Feminist Metaphysics*, ed. Charlotte Witt, (Dordrecht: Springer, 2011), 67–83; for an attempt to explain the relation of sex/gender categories in terms of the conferral of sex and gender, and the grounding of psychological and social qualities in (supposedly) biological ones, see Ásta Kristjana Sveinsdóttir, 'The Metaphysics of Sex and Gender', in *Feminist Metaphysics*, 47–65.

8. I should emphasise that this social reality can, of course, be subject to criticism: we need not accept a convention just because it exists.

9. Erik H. Erikson is the touchstone here; see his *Childhood and Society* (Harmondsworth, Middlesex: Penguin Books, 1965 [first published in 1950]) and 'Identity and the Life Cycle: Selected Papers', in *Psychological Issues*, vol. 1, ed. George S. Klein (New York: International Universities Press, 1959). For an overview of current research directions, see Dan P. McAdams and Kate C. McLean, 'Narrative Identity', *Current Directions in Psychological Science* 22:3 (2013), 233–238.

10. Alasdair MacIntyre, *After Virtue*, second edition (London: Duckworth, 1985), see esp. ch. 15 ('The Virtues, the Unity of a Human Life, and the Concept of a Tradition'); Charles Taylor, *Sources of the Self: The Making of the Modern Identity* (Cambridge: Cambridge University Press, 1989).

11. MacIntyre, *After Virtue*, 204–205.

12. Erving Goffman, *The Presentation of Self in Everyday Life* (London: Penguin Books, 1990, first published in 1959).

13. Interestingly, both MacIntyre and Galen Strawson (whose critique of narrativity I will discuss further) refer to Sarte's novel *La Nausée* and its main character Antoine Roquentin: MacIntyre disapprovingly, Strawson approvingly. For MacIntyre,

the character of Roquentin is a symptom of a modern sickness; for Strawson, he is a witness to his own anti-narrative view.

14. Taylor, *Sources of the Self*, 17.

15. Taylor, *Sources of the Self*, 26. In his 'The Politics of Recognition' (in *Multiculturalism*, ed. Amy Gutmann, Princeton: Princeton University Press, 1994, 25–73), Taylor explores this theme with particular attention to the damage that can be done when such identification is made difficult or impossible; in other words, when people are *misrecognized*. He says (26): 'Due recognition is not just a courtesy we owe people. It is a vital human need'.

16. Schechtman, *The Constitution of Selves*, 25.

17. Schechtman, *The Constitution of Selves*, 73.

18. Schechtman, *The Constitution of Selves*, 93.

19. MacIntyre, *After Virtue*, 207.

20. Schechtman, *Staying Alive*, 110–119.

21. Lindemann, *Holding and Letting Go*, chs. 3–5.

22. Galen Strawson, 'Against Narrativity', *Ratio* 17 (2004): 428–452.

23. Strawson, 'Against Narrativity', 436.

24. Schechtman addresses this worry, insofar as it could be directed against her earlier account from *The Constitution of Selves* in *Staying Alive*, 99–102.

25. This is suggested by J. David Velleman in 'Narrative Explanation', *The Philosophical Review* 112 (2003), 3. Velleman argues, however, that this 'explanatory force' is of an emotional nature and warns of a 'projective error' (20) that may occur when the audience of a narrative takes their emotional grasp of it (how they feel about the protagonists) as indication that they have understood the actual sequence of events. I will return to this problem of emotional bias further.

26. Hume, *Treatise*, sect. 1.3.14–15, 105–118.

27. Cf. Kant, *Critique of Pure Reason*, A94.

28. Hume, *Treatise*, sect. 1.4.6, 164.

29. Kant, *Critique of Pure Reason*, B132–140.

30. Strawson, 'Against Narrativity', 430.

31. Galen Strawson, 'I Am Not a Story', *Aeon*, 1 September 2015, accessed 2 October 2016: https://aeon.co/essays/let-s-ditch-the-dangerous-idea-that-life-is-a-story.

32. McAdams and McLean, 'Narrative Identity', 233.

33. Hume, *Treatise*, sect. 1.4.7, 175; fittingly this passage, the closing section of book I of the *Treatise*, follows right after his discussion of personal identity.

34. Schechtman, *Staying Alive*, 103.

35. Lindemann, *Holding and Letting Go*, 4.

36. Lindemann, *Holding and Letting Go*, 6.

37. Schechtman, *Staying Alive*, 114; Lindemann alludes to shared 'scripts' that people can invoke in performing their identities, *Holding and Letting Go*, 100–102.

38. Lynne Rudder Baker, 'Making Sense of Ourselves: Self-Narratives and Personal Identity', *Phenomenology and the Cognitive Sciences* 15 (2016), 11–12.

39. Schechtman, *Staying Alive*, 118.

40. Both Schechtman and Lindemann hold that children – even severely impaired children – and the demented can be persons under the narrative account; see Lindemann, *Holding and Letting Go*, chs. 1 and 5.

41. Goffman, *Presentation of Self*, 26.

42. J. C. Buitelaar, 'Privacy and Narrativity in the Internet Era', *The Information Society* 30:4 (2014), 272.

43. Even when someone reveals a negative aspect of their personality, the appropriate reaction in such a case would be disappointment, not the feeling of being deceived.

44. Joel Munsell (ed.), *Cases of Personal Identity*, Albany: Self-published, 1854.

45. Munsell, *Cases of Personal Identity*, 3–34.

46. For an instructive insight into the history of fingerprinting as a forensic practice, see Simon A. Cole, *Suspect Identities: A History of Fingerprinting and Criminal Identification* (Cambridge and London: Harvard University Press, 2001).

47. Cole, *Suspect Identities*, 89.

48. Schechtman, *Staying Alive*, 114.

49. Lindemann, *Holding and Letting Go*, 160–165.

50. Lindemann, *Holding and Letting Go*, 164.

51. Lindemann, *Holding and Letting Go*, 172.

52. These questions are discussed carefully and critically in David Lamb, 'Autonomy and the Refusal of Life-Prolonging Therapy', *Res Publica* 1:2 (1995), 147–162.

53. For a recent account that rejects bringing any narrative concerns into the debate, see Sabine Müller et al., 'Threats to Neurosurgical Patients Posed by the Personal Identity Debate', *Neuroethics*, online first (21 January 2017), doi: 10.1007/s12152-017-9304-0.

54. For an account that is very critical of contemporary anti-depressants and their emotional and social side effects, see Ian Gold and Lauren Olin, 'From Descartes to Desipramine: Psychopharmacology and the Self', *Transcultural Psychology* 46:1 (2009): 38–59; for an account that defends anti-depressants as an authentic form of 'self-enhancement', see David DeGrazia, 'Enhancement, and Self-Creation', *The Hastings Center Report* 30:2 (2000): 34–40.

55. See Gold and Olin, 'From Descartes to Desipramine': they focus on the effects anti-depressants can have on the romantic and sexual lives of patients in order to make their point that the concern that these drugs alter personalities should be taken seriously.

56. Lamb, 'Autonomy and the Refusal of Life-Prolonging Therapy', 156.

57. Cf. Lamb, 'Autonomy and the Refusal of Life-Prolonging Therapy', 159.

58. Schechtman calls this a 'reality constraint' on the narrative view, *Staying Alive*, 101.

59. For a summary of KI's role and an assessment of their responsibility in this case, see the external report by Sten Heckscher et al., *Karolinska Institutet and the Macchiarini Case: A Summary in English and Swedish* (Stockholm: E-Tryck AB, 2016), available at the Institute's homepage, accessed 2 October 2016, http://ki.se/sites/default/files/karolinska_institutet_and_the_macchiarini_case_summary_in_english_and_swedish.pdf.

60. Adam Ciralsky, 'The Celebrity Surgeon who Used Love, Money and the Pope to Scam an NBC News Producer', *Vanity Fair*, 5 January 2016, accessed 2 October

2016, http://www.vanityfair.com/news/2016/01/celebrity-surgeon-nbc-news-producer-scam.

61. Goffman, *Presentation of Self*, 28–29.

62. The alcoholic might tell themselves that they 'could stop at any time' – until a concerned friend succeeds in showing them how worrisome their habits have got; a person who feels like they 'don't belong' in a particular community – working-class academics or artists, for instance – could benefit greatly from a mentor that shares his or her own background acts as a role model. This does not imply that self-deception is always amenable to correction, but even so, it leaves an opportunity for others to adjust their behaviour toward the self-deceiver.

63. Velleman, 'Narrative Explanation', 20.

64. See, for instance, Kristen Schilt and Laurel Westbrook, 'Bathroom Battleground and Penis Panics', *Contexts* 14:3 (2015): 26–31.

65. Talia Mae Bettcher, 'Evil Deceivers and Make-Believers: On Transphobic Violence and the Politics of Illusion', *Hypatia* 22 (2007): 43–65.

66. Lizzie Dearden, 'German Solder Posing as Syrian Refugee Arrested for Planning "False Flag" Terror Attack', *The Independent*, 27 April 2017, accessed 31 May 2017, http://www.independent.co.uk/news/world/europe/german-soldier-syria-refugee-false-flag-terror-attack-posing-arrested-frankfurt-france-bavaria-a7705231.html.

67. The process is described on the U.S. State Department's homepage, accessed 31 May 2017, https://www.state.gov/j/prm/ra/admissions/.

68. Schechtman, *Staying Alive*, 103–104.

69. Schechtman, *Staying Alive*, 125–131.

70. Schechtman, *Staying Alive*, 125.

71. Schechtman, *Staying Alive*, 127. For if slaves or women were truly regarded as non-persons by slaveholders or misogynists, they would have no reason to think that there could be an intelligible conversation about what legal rights and duties slaves have, or about whether women should be allowed to vote. For a similar point about torture, see Bob Brecher, *Torture and the Ticking Bomb* (Malden: Blackwell, 2007), 78–79; Brecher emphasises that a torturer must first recognize a person *as a person* in order to break them by treating them like an object.

Chapter 3

Identity and Modern Statecraft

In the previous chapter, we looked at narrative accounts of identity and their detractors. Two main conclusions emerged from this analysis. First, official identities and administrative processes – and not just storytelling and communal rituals of remembrance – fit the narrative form. Second, identity is primarily a normative concept. As a descriptive concept, narrative identity would be vulnerable to the objection that it invites relativism: for insofar as it appears that any story counts, so long as it is told as a story, there seem to be no limits to what might be put forward as the relevant story. If narrativity is understood normatively, however, the perspective changes: we recognize that 'stories' emerge in a political and social environment shaped by power relations. On this view, identities are tied to communities, but the resulting recognition view need not be relativist – because oppressive and violent narratives can be ruled out. Official identity management is an expression of power relations and the site of political and moral conflicts. This means that rather than focusing on the alleged epistemic relativism of the narrative account, we need to consider its moral impact: when are stories used to silence and oppress people? When are they used to empower? More to the point of what follows in this chapter: Are the state's efforts in identity management merely an exercise in domination – or do they confer power and autonomy on individuals as well?

Towards the premature end of his life, Michel Foucault was thinking about 'technologies of the self', envisioning a historical study of practices by which people turned themselves into persons, that is, into subjects of agency and experience.[1] In one of the few preserved texts of this phase of his scholarship, he reflects on the 'political technology of individuals'.[2] As a historiographical piece, Foucault's text focuses on the rather obscure discipline of *Polizeiwissenschaft*, literally 'the science of policing'.[3] But the overarching theme of the piece is *raison d'état*. Foucault describes the modern state as an entity that takes itself as the reason and goal of its existence; and consequently its 'new art of governing is precisely not to reinforce the power [of monarchs or feudal lords and ladies]. Its aim is to reinforce the state itself.'[4]

This modern state comes with a new art of 'knowing' its subjects, and Foucault finds this knowledge exemplified in early modern, utopian visions of what *Polizeiwissenschaft* should be, namely the total administration of all aspects of the lives of individual citizens. The most curious aspect of Foucault's account of *raison d'état* is that this kind of reason must know its objects (the state's inhabitants) as individuals with their specific needs and skills, but needs to know them only insofar and inasmuch as they are of use to the state. The modern state's perspective is thus at the same time more detailed and narrower than that of its feudal predecessors. To give a concrete and somewhat simplified example: a medieval king or queen needed only to be assured of the loyalty of their noblemen for military purposes; it was they who would raise the armies for the kingdom and thereby wielded considerable political influence in the realm. The modern state, however, has a fundamentally different relation to its military. One of its most important inventions is the draft registry, which allows central administrators and officers to keep track of individual soldiers in its cities and counties. While the feudal realm needed only to 'see' relations within the nobility, the modern state aims to keep track of all its denizens. In the draft registry, these individuals are seen only according under a single category: whether they are fit to fight. The modern state 'invents' the individual person as an administrative unit, but this unit is defined narrowly in terms of the state's goals and intentions.

> Certain forms of knowledge and control require a narrowing of vision. The great advantage of such tunnel vision is that it brings into sharp focus certain limited aspects of an otherwise far more complex and unwieldy reality. This very simplification, in turn, makes the phenomenon at the center of the field of vision more legible and hence more susceptible to careful measurement and calculation. [An] overall, aggregate, synoptic view of a selective reality is achieved, making possible a high degree of schematic knowledge, control, and manipulation.[5]

In what follows, I will seek to understand the development of our contemporary regimes of identity management as an aspect of the history of modern technologies of the self. The narrowing of vision that belongs to this history can be read as an exercise of complete power and – with James C. Scott – as a scheme that follows a certain historical logic but is ultimately doomed to fail. I pursue both readings, but I shall suggest here and in the subsequent chapter that we do not have to accept Foucault's and Scott's pessimistic visions: the logic of modern statecraft and identity management bears serious moral risks, but under the right conditions and with proper watchfulness, it can indeed become a tool of autonomy.

3.1 'SEEING LIKE A STATE'

In his monumental study *Seeing Like a State*, James C. Scott describes modern statecraft as a project of legibility. Scott begins with Prussian forestry, discusses modern city planning – with a special focus on entirely planned cities like Brasilia and Chandigarh – and also touches upon the assignment of stable names and identities as a centrepiece of modern bureaucracy.[6] He notes that in all these undertakings, the modern, centralized state expresses a need to transform local, contextual knowledge into something that a central authority – removed from the source and context of this knowledge – can comprehend and regulate. Prussian foresters wanted woods whose yield and profitability could be measured on a simple scale, so they devised forestry monocultures.[7] City planning efforts broke up neighbourhoods that were seen as sources of chaos and unrest, or confusing and difficult for an outsider to navigate, and sought to impose order in the form of street grids and open spaces.[8] The assignment of permanent last names and the creation of registries are administrative interventions in the same spirit of legibility. In a small community where almost everyone knows each other personally, last names are unnecessary. Individuals can be referred to by nicknames or by their professions, and everyone in the community knows who they refer to.[9] But to an administrator, a tax collector or a draft officer, this local knowledge is of little use. The state and its institutions and agents cannot 'see' the people behind the local names. So once the state gets involved in the management of individual people at the local level, stable last names are needed; otherwise, the keeping of records for various state purposes is impossible. A telling example of the power of record-keeping is the public burning of draft records that occurred on 17 May 1968 in Catonsville, Maryland. The late Father Daniel Berrigan, SJ, his brother and seven other Catholic pacifists

> entered a Knights of Columbus building . . . and went up to the second floor, where the local draft board had offices. In front of astonished clerks, they seized hundreds of draft records, carried them down to the parking lot and set them on fire with homemade napalm.[10]

Their actions inspired similar acts of civil disobedience across the United States and the trial of the Catonsville Nine, as they were called, attracted international attention.[11] The burning of draft records and draft cards had an obvious symbolic element: resistance against a state that was waging a brutal and unjust war. But the burning of draft records – as opposed to the burning of draft cards – also disrupted the actual draft: without records – that is, without names and addresses – local draft boards would not know who to look for.

Standardized naming practices for individuals are not an administrative triviality, nor should the political power these practices both require and confer be underestimated. While the ancient Chinese Empire may have succeeded in imposing fixed surnames on its population as early as the fourth century BC, this process did not get under way in Europe until late medieval and early modern times, with the exception of names taken by the nobility and those kept in church records and early tax registries.[12] What church records started, modern bureaucracy perfected: records of births, marriages and deaths; passports; draft and voting registries. As societies begun to rely more and more on the state and its centralized bureaucracy for both legal acts (such as marriages) and social services (such as welfare), keeping records became a way of ensuring that people could function as citizens and legal persons. In this process identities were not merely being recorded, they were created by the state.[13] So let us turn to two examples where official naming practices and record-keeping quite obviously created new forms of identities: Ashkenazi Jewish surnames and the Nordic *personnummer* system.

Up until late medieval times, Jewish communities – like most other communities – primarily used patronymics and place names as specific identifiers. But these identifiers were not transmitted from parents to children; they were not stable family names as we know them now.[14] The first stable family names sprang up in medieval cities in Italy and among the Sephardic Jews of Spain and Portugal, when they were driven into exile. The Ashkenazi Jews of Central and Eastern Europe generally lived without surnames until the late eighteenth century, as they were much more isolated and marginalized communities than their Sephardic counterparts.[15] Yet when the Jews were 'emancipated' in the German states, the Austro-Hungarian Empire and the Russian Empire[16] at the end of the eighteenth and the first half of nineteenth centuries, the prize of their inclusion in civil society was the adoption of a fixed surname.

> These new regulations were intended, above all, to serve several practical ends for the governments concerned. The levying of taxes would be expedited by fixed surnames, and so would the conscription of Jewish soldiers. But here was also an opportunity to . . . assimilate the Jew. To many an 'enlightened' Jew himself, the adoption of a family name looked to be one more asset in the struggle to secure equal rights and integrate oneself in the Gentile world.[17]

The prize for integration was often a literal one, as clerks charged hefty fees for the privilege of adopting flowery family names such as Mandelbaum (almond tree) or telling ones such as Ehrlich (honest); while those who could not pay might end up with surnames like Garfunkel (or Garfinkel, carbuncle).[18] The imposition of family names on the Ashkenazi Jews achieved legibility in the sense that a centralized state could now record information about individuals in these communities without having to rely on local knowledge. It allowed the state to 'see' directly who was a member of these communities, and as such owed taxes or could be drafted into military service. Later, the legibility of these Jewish communities to the state became an instrument of terror and mass murder, as keeping records of these communities allowed for easier persecution, something which the Nazis readily exploited. Scott discusses a 1941 map of Amsterdam showing 'The Distribution of Jews in the Municipality' – based on detailed population records compiled by diligent Dutch civil servants – which helped the Nazi occupiers in their efforts to round up and deport the Jewish community of Amsterdam.[19]

The imposition of surnames on the Ashkenazi Jews is but one chapter of a slow but steady development that marks the transformation of pre-modern communities and feudal states into modern bureaucracies. A crucial feature of this transformation was the replacement of local knowledge with regionally and nationally useful knowledge. This is evident in the decline of patronymics, matronymics and other changeable bynames as the primary way of identifying persons in many European languages. To my knowledge, Iceland is the only European country in which the legal name of a person is still formed by a patronymic or matronymic, and where there are no hereditary family names.[20] For instance, if an Icelandic man named Bjarnar Guðmundsson has a daughter named Helga, then her legal name would be Helga Bjarnadóttir; and if she has a son named Halldór, then his legal name would be Halldór Helgason. In other Scandinavian languages, as in other European languages, patronymics eventually became stable surnames. This is evident in common surnames like the Swedish Johansson, the Norwegian and Danish Hansen or the Dutch Jozefzoon; and in more obscure forms like the German Brüning (derived from 'Bruno' and the old Germanic suffix '-ing') or the Welsh Bevan (derived from 'Evan' and the prefix 'ap-'). Other common ways in which bynames evolved into stable family names included the transgenerational stabilization of occupational names (Baker, Smith), place names (Hill, Rivers) or nicknames.[21] In many places in Europe, this transformation began in medieval towns, where population growth necessitated the use of bynames to identify people; some family names – the famous Rothschild among them – can be traced back to the use of painted shields to identify houses: Rothschild comes from the red shield that once marked the family home.

The standardization of naming practices is an important tool of modern statecraft, indicating a significant shift in identification and recognition practices. In a medieval village, it was enough for virtually all purposes that some is known as 'Mary Rivers' or 'John Smith'. This principle still holds today in intimate contexts and communities: in families, and among friends or colleagues in a small firm, the use of a single name or a nickname typically suffices to refer to someone without ambiguity. Yet even among nicknames, we can find significant variation and overlap and thus potential for confusion. Russian has one of the most refined and complicated linguistic mechanisms for the formation of affectionate nicknames (*hypocoristics*). We can find a number of different variations of one name: Tolya, Tol'ka, Tolechka, Tolen'ka, Tolyukha, Tolyusha, Tolyushka and Tolyuchenka are all variations of the proper name Anatoliy, expressing different levels of familiarity and endearment;[22] we can find hypocoristics that apply to different names of different genders: Polya can be an affectionate form of both Apolloniy and Polina; and we have hypocoristics that also occur as their own proper names: Sasha for Aleksandr or Nadya for Nadezhda or Ksen'ya for Aksin'ya.[23] The proper use of nicknames – both in Russian and in languages which have a less developed infrastructure for hypocoristics – is heavily dependent on context and regulated by social convention and personal preference.[24] The identity narratives attached to these names were firmly rooted in their local context, and comparatively few people ever left this immediate context. For those who did, the wider world of course offered more opportunities for anonymity and for – quite literally – starting a new life than it does today. It is no coincidence that Simon Cole's study on the history of forensic fingerprinting begins with the story of Martin Guerre, whom we already encountered. As Cole puts it: 'Martin Guerre posed a problem of identification precise because he had been "snatched from the context of fields and family" for eight years'.[25]

With the advent of modern statecraft, local, contextual knowledge came under pressure from a centralized, national administration. Both citizens and the state now increasingly relied on the use of names that served as unique identifiers across different local communities; a development that went hand in hand with increasing social and geographical mobility in the wake of industrialization and the ensuing *Landflucht* of the eighteenth and nineteenth centuries and the formation of the modern metropolis.[26] Today, this development continues with the implementation of technologically mediated forms of identity management, which supplement or replace the use of names, photographs and paper-based records with digital identifiers and biometric markers. A particularly interesting example in this regard is the Nordic 'personal number' system, which combines total bureaucracy and technocracy.

3.2 THE PERSONAL NUMBER

In Norway, Sweden, Denmark, Finland and Iceland, every citizen and legal resident has a personal identification number; either assigned to them at birth, or in the case of immigrants, applied for when they take up legal residence. In Sweden, this *personnummer* was first introduced as an identifier in 1947 and its current format dates from 1967 and consists of ten digits: the birth date in YYMMDD-format and an extension of four digits. The first three digits of the extension are the 'birth number' (*födelsenummer*) that is always odd for men and even for women, while the last digit of the extension is a control number. Until 1990, the 'birth number' also reflected the county (*län*) of birth; since then, it has been randomly drawn from a nationwide pool of numbers.[27]

The *personnummer* functions as a unique identifier across multiple contexts: it is used in the total population registry (*Registret över totalbefolkningen*, RTB), in the tax registry, the national social security system, the health care system, and in the driving licence and passport registries.[28] Even many private businesses require it; and when picking up a package from the post office or prescription medicine from the pharmacy, the clerk would typically just ask for your 'last four digits' when they already have figured the first half of your *personnummer* from the birth date on your ID-card or passport. The *personnummer*, together with other information kept in the population registry, such as name and address, is treated as public information in Sweden.[29] This is true for the other Nordic countries as well; in Iceland, anyone can, with some effort, deduce the *kennitala* (Icelandic counterpart of the *personnummer*) from a given name and vice versa.[30] Its near-universal use, its interoperability and its status as public information distinguish the *personnummer* from similar identifiers in Europe and North America. For privacy reasons, Germany uses different personal identification numbers for its pension and health care systems, and there is no national population registry. The British National Insurance Number is used only for health care and social security and required only for British citizens over sixteen years of age and for international employees. The American Social Security Number is used for both social security and taxation, but the U.S. Social Security Administration advises its customers to treat the number as strictly confidential information in order to minimize the risk for identity theft.[31] In stark contrast, the Nordic systems were actually designed for maximum transparency and maximum identifiability; there is no firewall between different government agencies, nor between private and public contexts in which the personal identification number is used.[32]

In a sense, personal identification numbers are the logical next step for institutions that need to identify a vast number of clients without delay or ambiguity. Two-part and three-part naming systems, as they are now customary in most parts of the world, do not, of course, guarantee that everyone will have a unique identifier – even with additional data, this might not always be guaranteed. Two John Smiths might have the same birth date and birthplace and would need to be differentiated by even more information. Personal identification numbers, on the other hand, can be used as truly unique identifiers that establish solid administrative links between a person, their name(s), date of birth, address(es), employment and tax records, medical records and social security records.[33] Scandinavians typically place a lot of trust in this system,[34] and they rarely seem to consider the risks of the system's transparency or how entrenched the use of personal identification numbers is in their countries. The personal number is a crucial element of communication between citizens and the state, as well as between citizens – for instance, in business transactions where citizens do not know each other personally – and it is legal proof of residency.[35] It would be too simplistic to describe the trust in the *personnummer* as a mere extension of Scandinavians' trust in their well-oiled and benevolent welfare states and of their culture of transparency. The personal number system has obvious advantages in terms of making bureaucratic and economic interactions run more smoothly, and it actually serves to *build trust* between administrators and their customers.[36] Those who receive a personal number get legal identification that serves them their entire lives and across multiple contexts: they use it when they file their taxes, go to the doctor, apply for a passport, apply for a loan from their bank or even when they buy a new mobile phone. Those who serve them, in turn, can trust that the same identifier will be used in the tax registry and show up on their medical records or on their driver's licence – that is, they know that the *personnummer* links the person in front of him or her to a vast network of background information.

The *personnummer* also has advantages for scientists who work with statistical or epidemiological data. An article on the use of the *personnummer* in health care and research notes:

> Large medical databases such as the Swedish Cancer Register or the Swedish Patient Register, built around the [personal identification number], create additional value to society. The PIN enables researchers to merge such registers and to examine an array of questions, including the long-term consequences of preterm birth or . . . the medical consequences of alcohol abuse, or the association between a medical event and human behavior. . . . Such research will not only optimize health care resource allocation but more importantly improve the management of both current and future patients. Through the PIN it is possible to trace virtually any patient. The medical outcome of the patient . . . can be used to evaluate sensitivity and specificity of new diagnostic techniques tested on both historic and new blood samples. Finally, the natural course of the disease (as recorded in registers and patient charts) serves to educate medical students.[37]

The authors further argue that there are no privacy concerns about the fact that medical records and different medical databases are so easily linked and information so easily accessed by a vast number of health care professionals – indeed, they claim that 'the current situation [in which patients have virtually no opportunity to prevent the use of their records for research] benefits patients and society, and that informed consent should not be required for large-scale medical research'.[38] What might seem a privacy nightmare – I suspect that German bioethicists especially would have serious issues with this view – does have actual advantages. For instance, prescriptions do not require paper slips: the doctor can file a record of the prescription online, which is attached to the *personnnummer* and can be viewed by any pharmacist in Sweden. This reduces the risk for fraud or misunderstandings, and it allows the patient to use any pharmacy to pick up their medicine.

In addition to privacy concerns, however, the system has an even more concerning downside: since it is so comprehensive and so widely used and accepted, it excludes those who cannot obtain a *personnummer* – and generates a class of non-persons, who remain invisible to the state and all other agents who rely on the state's identity management efforts. Temporary residents, vagrants and undocumented immigrants and some refugees fall into this category. Only persons who intend to take up residence in Sweden for more than a year are entitled to receive a *personnummer*;[39] and while short-term residents can apply for a coordination number (*samordningsnummer*) instead of a *personnummer*,[40] the *samordningsnummer* provides less social power.

An exchange student, for instance, would at most be entitled to receive a *samordningsnummer*; but this identifier immediately outs them as a short-term resident to prospective landlords or to banks – and Swedish landlords and banks typically insist that their tenants and customers possess a *personnummer*. For exchange students, this means that they will not be able to open a bank account or rent an apartment on the open market – in fact, most exchange students are dependent either on university housing, which is relatively scarce, or on the massive and exploitative black housing market in Sweden.[41] The situation is worse for unauthorized, paperless immigrants: without a *personnummer*, they are cut off from all communication with the state and most public institutions and cannot participate in public life, nor access basic services. As Erika Sigvardsdotter notes in her dissertation on this topic, the universal reliance on the *personnummer* has made it 'in many cases... *technically* impossible for a receptionist or cashier to serve a person who cannot produce an ID-number, or for a doctor to create a medical recording in their name'.[42] That is, even where professionals want to help an undocumented migrant, they are prevented from doing so by the *personnummer* system.

If we apply Scott's concept of 'seeing like a state' to the *personnummer*, we can describe it as follows: the personal identification number is an extension of the modern administrative project to make citizens 'legible' to the state. It does this by linking each individual to a unique administrative history, including residency and taxpayer status, medical data or employment history. For those who are entitled to trace these linkages, both the individual and larger societal trends become transparent: it is no accident that Swedish researchers emphasize that the *personnummer* system provides them with a unique opportunity to study complex societal issues.[43] Due to its comprehensiveness and its interoperability, it also has clear advantages in terms of trustworthiness – that is, in terms of the background information linked to each *personnummer*, which ensures that it is a genuine identifier for each person. It would be wrong, however, simply to view the *personnummer* system as a tool of dominance and surveillance. It is a *technology of power* in that it allows institutions and agents of the state to track people and to record and process intimate details of their lives. But it is also a *technology of the self*, by which the subject can assert themselves as an individual in their dealings with the state and can claim his or her rights. The same technology that allows the state to track you also allows you to prove your identity as a citizen or legal resident, as a taxpayer and as someone who is entitled to health care or to drive a car. Identity management systems can, of course, be turned against their subjects – this will be the topic of the next chapter. But we should be careful not to view all innovation in the field of identity management under the perspective of disciplining and surveillance.

3.3 WHOSE POWER?

There is a new generation of sociologists and criminologists whose work is particularly concerned with the expanding use of biometrics in security and identification schemes.[44] Much of this work is inspired by David Lyon, who transformed surveillance into a major issue for sociologists;[45] and both Lyon and the new generation often explicitly refer to Foucault – specifically, to Foucault's understanding of the *Panopticon*, the structure in which an unseen observer surveils a group of prisoners and keeps them docile.[46] Much of this work focuses on the *biological* aspect of biometric identification – that is, the fact that biometric identification is dependent on and inflicted on human bodies; and many critical analyses in this field start from the observation that the same biometric capacities that are used to make identification routines more convenient for some are used to restrict the movement of others.[47] In the European Union, we have a high-quality and high-security biometric passport, which confers travel privileges to those who possess one – my German passport gives me visa-free access to 177 countries – but we also have the EURODAC database, which stores the fingerprints of asylum-seekers entering the Union, and whose purpose is to track and restrict the movement of these asylum-seekers. Thus, someone who was already registered in Italy and then travels to Germany and again applies for asylum can be deported to Italy on the basis of their previous application.[48]

In my view, however, this critical literature makes too much of the role of the body in these schemes and too little of the nuances and gaps in the actual administrative practices of identification and identity verification. To my knowledge, none of the sociologists and criminologists, who, broadly speaking, work in an Anglophone tradition inspired by Foucault, have considered the Nordic personal identification numbers in any detail – even though this system is, as we saw, more comprehensive than any identification scheme building primarily on biometric markers. Instead, they focus on the symbolic importance of incorporating bodily features in identification practices, such that persons who want or need to participate in biometric identification are required to 'give up a piece of themselves'.[49] This focus on the bodily components of biometric identity management, however, can obscure the perspective on the distinctly modern logic that undergirds these practices and the different ways in which this logic manifests itself.

Btihaj Ajana describes biometric technology

> as a means of facilitating and automating the triage of identities through identification and authentication. . . . It is a way of organising and categorizing individual and collective biovalue by opening up the body to various economically driven processes.[50]

This is wrong in two ways. First it reduces identity management to the management of 'biovalue', thus ignores any positive value that legal identification can provide. Second, it presumes that there is an existing pool of identities – some desirable, some undesirable – which is sorted with the help of biometric markers. Given the recognition view of identity that I have argued for, it would be more accurate to say that the use of biometrics can help *create* identities. But the creation of identities does not necessitate the use of biometrics; it does not need to be 'written on the body',[51] as these scholars dramatically announce. In the case of, say, a paperless Syrian refugee who arrives on a Greek island and is fingerprinted by local police, it would be more apt to say that this process creates an identity which European authorities can 'read'. The process itself, however, says nothing about the actual or presumed 'biovalue' of the refugee, for whatever value will be assigned to their story and his or her claim to protection will be decided largely in terms of narrative evidence, not in terms of their biometric features.[52] At most, the fingerprints might expose them as an asylum-seeker who can be returned to another 'safe' country – if they have submitted an application for asylum elsewhere in the European Union. This is not to say that refugees are not widely treated as undesirables or that there is no arbitrary state violence inflicted on them.

But this is hardly a direct result of the use of biometrics – it is the result of features that are ascribed to refugees as members of specific social groupings. We will take a closer look at the role of social identities in further section and in the next chapter; for now, I want to stress that it is not 'the body' as such that is the focus of restrictive policies, nor is 'the body' even necessary for such policies.

Contemporary biometrics is a new tool of identification, not an entirely new form of identity management: using bodily features for purposes of re-identification is nothing new. What is new is the specific features that are being used and the degree to which their use has been standardized – drawings or vague physical descriptions of people have become biometric passport photographs that must conform to a specific layout. The ways in which power is exercised through the use of biometry, however, is not determined by the technology itself – it is determined by political will and resistance. The political ambition to create detailed records of all the people and all the assets that belong to a state is arguably a modern one. But it is modern in a seventeenth- to nineteenth-century-sense, not in a twentieth- or twenty-first-century sense.[53] New technologies offer states new possibilities of registration and control – but the will to register and control is not dependent on the emergence of a particular technology. Nor is every security technology used only for purposes of domination. Those who study security systems tend to focus on the ways in which a given infrastructure coerces people: a biometric scanner denies someone entry; refugees are subjected to an administrative process that is reminiscent of police work; a fence is erected in order to protect a piece of land or an international border. But contemporary security infrastructure often combines control with access: biometric identification can give me (privileged) access to a building or a country; the refugee who has been fingerprinted and registered can now access social services.

Along similar lines, I suspect that the Nordic *personnummer* system is so widely accepted and so powerful, because it also works in the service of individuals who, in virtue of having a unique and interoperable legal identity, can assert their individuality in their dealings with the state and claim their rights and eligibility for specific services.[54] Conversely, I doubt that the personal identification number would have been so successful in these democratic states, if it were merely an instrument of control. Nevertheless, the downside of this system is that it privileges a *particular* form of standardized knowledge and so renders people who do not have access to the use of this knowledge invisible. For the agents of the state, these persons become indecipherable and the state's institutions become blind to them. What I want to emphasize here, however, is that any system of centralized identity registration follows a certain internal logic that can be described as distinctively modern in ambition and in execution. Central national registries, social security numbers, *personnummer*, tax-IDs and perhaps in the future centralized archives of genetic data:[55] all of these are not only *technologies of power* but also *technologies of the self*; and they not only serve to control and dominate but also to provide intelligible ways for individuals to assert themselves – their identity – beyond the circles of the local and the intimate. They offer the option of a narrative of the self that is not bound and limited by personal knowledge and personal recognition. They are narrative technologies for living among strangers.

3.4 IDENTITIES AS BRANDS

In his study of modern nationalism, *Imagined Communities*,[56] Benedict Anderson offers a broad analysis of the roots of modern European nationalism and its post-colonial successors in Africa and Asia. While it is not possible here to discuss Anderson's work in depth, I want to highlight one chapter that suggests interesting parallels with Scott's analysis of modern statecraft and lets us view passports and official identities generally as linked to the enterprise of nation-building. With Anderson, passports can be understood as logos or brands, which connect the individual to the national grouping they belong to.

In chapter ten of *Imagined Communities*, Anderson discusses censuses, maps and museums[57] as tools of European nation-builders and their post-colonial successors. He takes examples primarily from South East Asia, from English and Dutch colonial administrations and the Kingdom of Siam. Of particular interest here are Anderson's discussions of maps and censuses, since they illustrate how the creation of administrative tools is simultaneous with the categories they purport to capture: the drawing of a map makes the territory of a nation; and a nation-wide census makes people into particular kinds of citizens, with a specific religion or ethnicity. Maps and censuses thus create normative categories – such as the ascription of religious or ethnic traits – under the guise of representing a complete, objective view of reality. According to Anderson, the most significant innovation of European census-takers in colonized lands was 'not in the *construction* of ethnic-racial classifications but rather in the systematic *quantification*',[58] for it was this quantification that allowed them to impart an objective air to these classifications – not unlike the way in which modern biology and psychology imparted an air of objectivity to social gender norms. A clear parallel emerges with Scott's analysis of the totalizing but shallow view of the administrators of modern statecraft. Racial and ethnic categories were present before the colonizers arrived, but it was the colonizers who made them into comprehensive means of 'seeing', thus controlling their subjects – and the political and social legacy of this categorization is in many places still painfully present.

Map-making can be understood similarly. Anderson describes the map as a kind of brand or logo for modern nation-states. This brand-like character is evident in colonial-era maps, with fixed colours assigned to each colonial power: Great Britain in red, France in blue, Portugal in green and Spain in gold. 'Dyed in this way, the colony appeared like a detachable piece of a jigsaw puzzle. As the "jigsaw" effect became normal, each "piece" could be wholly detached from its geographic context.'[59] Thus the national map and the colonial map become a logotype for the nation; they project the nation-state's claims to territory and to legitimacy onto an abstract, two-dimensional plane. This perspective views the landscape from above, a view alien to those who actually inhabit the land or travel across it.

> [As a logotype] the map entered an infinitely reproducible series, available for transfer to posters, official seals, letterheads, magazine and textbook covers, tablecloths, and hotel walls. Instantly recognizable, everywhere visible, the logo-map penetrated deep into the popular imagination.[60]

The passport, too, can also be seen as a logotype or a brand. Not only does it often contain symbols that are important to each nation's imagined identity – take, for instance, Eire's harp or Germany's *Bundesadler* on the cover; or fanciful designs on the pages, such as in the new Norwegian passport, which feature simplified images of the country's natural beauty. The passport also brands its holder as a member of an imagined community, for better or for worse; thus, it communicates national identity and personal identification at the same time. It is an administrative combination of personal and social identity. This was not always the case. When passports first became a means of identification in the modern era, they were literally pass-ports: an official permission to pass through a sovereign territory. Such pass-ports were primarily issued to foreigners (traders or diplomats), but not meant for citizens.[61] Things changed dramatically during and after the First World War:

> The (re)imposition of passport controls by numerous West European countries and the United States during the First World War and their persistence after the war was an essential aspect of that '*révolution identificatoire*' that vastly enhanced the ability of government to identify their citizens, to distinguish them from non-citizens, and thus to construct themselves as 'nation-states'.[62]

While passports today are symbols of the ability and the entitlement to travel to a foreign country of one's choosing, it is sometimes forgotten that passports also have a history of keeping people from leaving. This history is not limited to oppressive regimes and illiberal states – although it is certainly more developed there. The U.S. Passport Office under Ruth Shipley, who led the institution from 1928 until 1955, had a reputation for using the denial of a passport to keep citizens whose travel was not in the 'national interest' from leaving the country.[63] Among the prominent victims of Shipley's zeal were chemist Linus Pauling and playwright Arthur Miller, whose passport applications were stalled due to their political leanings.[64] Their cases remind us that passports are a means to control the movement of not only foreigners but also of a state's own citizens – and to prevent them from travelling abroad when they seem 'untrustworthy'. Using passports in this way, however, depended on a shift from a document issued to foreign visitors to one issued to a state's own citizens.

The political urgency of this shift became clearly visible after the First World War. When the passport had become a general requirement for international travel, and when nationality had become the category by which to distinguish friends from enemies, denying people a passport – thus a nationality – became a political weapon. In 1921, after the end of the Russian Civil War, the Soviet government passed a decree that left millions of Russian refugees and emigrants – who had been stranded outside the Soviet Union in the wake of revolution and war – stateless. Without a nationality, however, these persons could not move within Europe, and the Soviet Union would not take them back. In response to the crisis, the explorer and philanthropist Fridtjof Nansen persuaded the League of Nations to issue special identity documents to these stateless people, which became known as the 'Nansen passport'.[65] The Nansen passport was later also issued to Armenians and other minorities who were persecuted and left stateless in the new Turkish Republic that had succeeded the collapsing Ottoman Empire.

After the Second World War, the problem of stateless persons re-emerged. The defeat of the Nazis and the liberation of the concentration camps had stranded hundreds of thousands of persons – most of them Jewish – in Germany. The displaced persons (DPs) as they were called then were no longer welcome in their countries of origin – if these countries still existed – and they were not welcome in the countries of the liberators (the United Kingdom, the United States, Australia and Canada) either. A concentration camp in Northern Germany, Bergen-Belsen, became a focal point of these conflicts. Immediately after the liberation of Bergen-Belsen in April 1945, British forces turned the concentration camp and the nearby army barracks in Bergen-Hohne into an administrative centre for the processing of DPs in the British Occupied Zone. Bergen-Belsen became one of the largest DP camps in post-war Germany and remained in operation until 1951. One problem encountered by the British administrators was that classifying DPs according to their nationality did not necessarily solve the problem of what to do with them: a Lithuanian, for instance, could not simply be 'repatriated', for their country no longer existed – indeed, if someone gave their nationality as Lithuanian, it might be an indication that they would not fare well if they were sent back to the Soviet Union.

The camp housed many Polish and other Eastern European forced labourers who had been deported to Germany during the war. While many of these could be sent back to their countries of origin without problems, Bergen-Belsen also housed over 20,000 Eastern European Jews, most of them Polish, who refused repatriation. These Jews had had been taken from their homes and their families, and they were still faced with violent anti-Semitism in Poland.[66] The British liberators, however, were not eager to let these Jews emigrate to the United Kingdom or other Commonwealth nations, nor did they want to let them go to Palestine and join the Zionist cause for an independent Israel. Consequently, they initially refused to recognize 'Jewish' as the national identity of these DPs, and only after considerable activism on behalf of the Jewish political organizations that had sprung up in the camp did they budge on this refusal. The situation of the Jewish DPs shows how nationality had become another crucially modern way of 'seeing' people: If 'Jewish' was not to be recognized as a nationality for geopolitical reasons, and if the other nationalities that might be assigned to the survivor were not viable destinations for repatriation, then the British authorities could not 'see' what to do with these people – and the DPs continued to be stuck in the middle of the country that had tried to exterminate them.

The logic of administrative 'seeing' that emerges here is one to which we will need to return, for it is one of the most dangerous aspects of modern identity management: instead of trying to make the individual legible as an individual, it understands the person exclusively as a member of a group. Where this group is marked as undesirable or dangerous, administrative consternation – in this case, about where to send the DPs – can turn into state-sanctioned violence. Understanding nationality – and by extension passports – as 'brands' or 'logotypes' makes this connection clear: where a biometric passport supported by a trustworthy national 'brand name' confers travel privilege and relative immunity from hostile questioning by border guards and police, the holder of an untrustworthy passport – marked by an undesirable or 'risky' nationality – or the stateless person trigger administrative confusion; or worse, administrative alarm. When we turn to more recent events in the next chapter, we will look at President Trump's 'Muslim ban' as one instance of the latter.

3.5 HIGH MODERNISM AND POSTMODERNISM

Let us now briefly return to Scott's study of modern statecraft: his central tenet is to urge caution when it comes to political ambitions to solve social problems by 'one-size-fits-all' solutions that operate on the grandest possible scale of statecraft. For Scott, Communist planned economies are paradigm cases of the failure of such solutions, for they must ignore vital local knowledge. His interest lies mainly in the way in which modern states have struggled against pre-modern ways of knowing and doing things: as one historical example of this, he cites the troubles land surveyors encountered in imposing the requirements of cadastral mapping – namely that it assign all land in a village to a particular holder – on rural areas that had communal traditions of land use or were using the land in ways that were not amenable to economic categorization.[67] When the cadastral map succeeded as the standardized and universally legible way of 'seeing' the land, pre-modern forms of agriculture slowly disappeared.

In identity management, administrators faced similar challenges: the imposition of standardized naming systems, for instance, rarely went smoothly and without resistance. This struggle continues, although in Western countries, it now mostly seems to be a fight against post-modern complications of and resistance to the state's ambition to impose unambiguous criteria for identifying and re-identifying people. This owes, in part, to the fact that many more people today enjoy freedom of movement – both between geographical areas and between different social groupings. This alone makes the project of 'fixing' people in their legal identities more ambitious and more difficult.

Take as an example the concerns about international terrorism that have had a tight grip on identity management and the security community since the 9/11 attacks on the United States. Since that day, air traffic security, border security and the perceived threats of immigration have become dominant issues in the political consciousness and the day-to-day political discourse of many Western states.[68] As part of this changed political consciousness, sweeping innovations were made to international travel documents. Due mainly to American pressure, the biometric, machine-readable passport became the global minimum standard for these documents. These passports store biometric information about the traveller on a chip; information which can be matched against live biometric data read by a scanner (e.g., integrated in an automated border gate). I do not want to discuss the privacy aspects of this innovation here;[69] I want to discuss whether it has failed along the same lines as the 'schemes' discussed in Scott's study have failed, namely in light of their own grand ambitions.

The global implementation of a passport format with fingerprint templates is a nice illustration of the high-modernist spirit. A 'one-size-fits-all' solution, supposedly leading to a significant increase in border and air traffic security and efficiency; pursued, arguably, with sincere political concerns in mind; and a solution which, over time, might usher in a benevolent global regime of identity management. But what has become of this vision fifteen years later? Few countries actually use the fingerprint information on biometric passports consistently; one of the few that does is the United States. In the European Union, this information is used only at the outside borders of the Schengen Area, and then only regarding travellers who are not citizens of the EU. International travel within the Schengen Area is still largely exempted from identity checks.[70] Yet most of those who were involved in acts of terror in Europe in the past decade were EU citizens, including those with an allegedly Islamist motivation. As EU citizens, these terrorists were exempt from many security schemes implemented to protect the Union's external borders and internal borders posed no hindrance to them. Recent indications of how ineffective the supposedly comprehensive security schemes to protect the European Union actually are in the light of this particular threat is the eventual capture of Salah Abdeslam, who could hide in Brussels for months after his involvement in the November 2015 attacks on Paris that claimed over 120 lives; and the flight of Anis Amri, who was responsible for the attack on the Christmas market on the Breitscheidplatz in Berlin in December 2016. Not only was Amri able to travel through Germany, France and Italy before he was eventually killed in a standoff with police in Milan, he had been imprisoned in Italy before he came to Germany as an asylum-seeker; and in Germany, he had been observed by police, but never detained.[71]

So why do such things keep happening, despite the heightened fear of terrorism and despite efforts to make identification management ever more secure? One reason – in the cases of Abdeslam and Amri – is poor communication between different police agencies and intelligence services – that is, information that cumulatively might mark these people as suspicious enough for an arrest or a closer investigation is never pooled. But the current focus on police work and the potential of asylum-seekers to be or turn into terrorists should not let us overlook the security loopholes of the identity documents themselves. The EU passport is one of the most 'trustworthy' identity documents in the world. Its security features make it virtually impossible to forge. But still, it is not immune to fraud. One weak spot of the passport is the issuance process: to apply for a passport, applicants need to provide so-called breeder documents, such as birth certificates or national ID cards. Often, these documents have much lower security standards than the passport and are much easier to forge – enabling a would-be fraudster to apply for a genuine passport with a fake birth certificate.[72] The problem becomes exponentially more challenging when we consider the possibility to apply for an EU passport in a country other than one's birth country – that is, a country where officials might be entirely unfamiliar with what a genuine birth certificate looks like.

The other weak spot is the potential for photograph fraud.[73] Within the Schengen Area, which is largely co-extensive with the European Union, the standard procedure for identity checks of EU citizens is simple visual inspection – although face recognition technology is available and evolving. Moreover, only a few countries within the European Union mandate that citizens must have their photo taken as they submit their passport application – in many places, they can bring their own, as long as it conforms to the general layout specifications. Furthermore, within the Schengen Area, national ID cards from EU member states are valid legal identification for international travel. This opens up two avenues for fraud: One is to simply lend the passport to a lookalike and travel with one's national ID card. The other is to digitally manipulate a photo provided for a passport. Since passports are valid for up to ten years, facial recognition – both in-person and machine-based – must allow a margin for natural aging, and this is what makes lookalike fraud possible.

So why are these loopholes not eliminated? In the broadest possible terms, I think it is because the modern state – and its high-modern project of complete identification and identifiability – clash with the messy realities of a post-modern world. Post-modern, as I use it here, is to be understood as a refusal – implicit or explicit – to be ascribed a fixed identity, and an endorsement of attitudes or practices that undercut such ascriptions. 'Queer', for instance, is a distinctly post-modern term in that it rejects the assumption that people are 'just' men or women or 'just' hetero- or homosexual. We could describe many aspects of the world we live in as post-modern in the sense that many people now have the opportunity to embody more than one identity category, to play with these categories, thus to resist being viewed as merely one thing or the other. A pious Catholic, for instance, might also be an openly gay person; a man might be also be the birth mother to his child; and someone who speaks English with an American accent need not be American – whereas someone who speaks with an accent other than American could be.

Post-modern flexibility about social identities makes the business of identity management more challenging, even more so where this post-modernism expresses itself as political resistance. Privacy concerns – which are co-responsible for some of the loopholes discussed above – can be described as post-modern in this sense: they express a refusal to be legible for the state at all times and in all places. This is not to say that these privacy concerns should not be taken seriously, or that loopholes ought to be fixed by more control and more surveillance. Some of the gaps in modern security architectures are simple design flaws and some are due to lack of communication and interoperability between national architectures, as in the breeder document scenario sketched earlier. In any case, we need to keep in mind that if a comprehensive identity management scheme is in place, it can be turned against those it is supposed to serve. This will be the topic of the next chapter.

NOTES

1. Preliminary reflections on this unfinished project are preserved in *Technologies of the Self: A Seminar with Michel Foucault*, ed. Luther. H. Martin et al. (London: Tavistock Publications 1988). This volume contains notes from Foucault and faculty members of the University of Vermont, where Foucault held a seminar on his new ideas in the autumn term of 1982.

2. Michel Foucault, 'The Political Technology of Individuals', in *Technologies of the Self*, 145–162.

3. Foucault claims ('The Political Technology of Individuals', 153) that at least in early modernity and during the Enlightenment, the German *Polizei* and the French *police* had a much broader meaning than their English counterpart.

4. Foucault, 'The Political Technology of Individuals', 150. For a similar observation about the role of *policing* in early modernity, see Nikolas Rose, *Governing the Soul: The Shaping of the Private Self*, second edition, (London and New York: Free Association Books, 1999), 225–226.

5. Scott, *Seeing Like a State*, 11.

6. Scott, *Seeing Like a State*, 53–84 and 103–146.

7. Scott, *Seeing Like a State*, 11–22. As Scott points out, this ecological experiment in central planning, which started out as a 'resounding success' became a failure in many places when the foresters realized a century later that their monocultures had disrupted the ecosystem of the soil in such a way that yields dropped dramatically.

8. Scott, *Seeing Like a State*, 53–58. He names the city of Bruges, with its medieval maze of narrow alleys, as an example of the pre-modern city and Chicago, with its gridiron layout, as an example of the modern city, in which getting around did no longer depend on having local knowledge.

9. Scott (*Seeing Like A State*, 64) illustrates this with an observation about the movie *Witness*, in which a police detective needs a local guide in order to successfully locate someone in the Amish community, since the Amish are not registered in phone books and have only a small set of last names. Scott notes: '[The police detective's] quandary reminds us that the great variety of surnames and given names in the United States allows us to identify unambiguously a large number of individuals whom we have never met'.

10. Daniel Lewis, 'Daniel J. Berrigan, Defiant Priest Who Preached Pacifism, Dies at 94', *New York Times*, 30 April 2016, accessed 21 March 2017, https://www.nytimes.com/2016/05/01/nyregion/daniel-j-berrigan-defiant-priest-who-preached-pacifism-dies-at-94.html?_r=0.

11. George Mische, 'Inattention to Accuracy about "Catonsville Nine" Distorts History', *National Catholic Reporter*, published online 17 May 2013, accessed 21 March 2017, https://www.ncronline.org/news/peace-justice/inattention-accuracy-about-catonsville-nine-distorts-history.

12. An early English example is the *Domesday Book* of 1086, which was created on orders of William the Conqueror. Stephanie Barker et al. – in *An Atlas of English Surnames* (Frankfurt am Main: Peter Lang 2007) – suggest that by 'about 1350, almost everyone in England had a hereditary name' (10) but it took until 1450

in Northern England and until the nineteenth century in remote parts of Wales for fixed surnames to become entrenched. Max Gottschald – in *Deutsche Namenskunde: Unsere Familiennamen (German Onomastics: Our Family Names)*, 5th improved edition with an introduction by Rudolf Schützeichel (Berlin and New York: Walter de Gruyter, 1982), 47 – writes that the same process in the German lands took from the twelfth century until 1600, moving from the West and South towards Eastern Europe.

13. The theme has been explored artistically in José Saramago's novel, *All the Names*, whose protagonist is a clerk in an enormous 'Central Registry of Births, Marriages and Deaths', trans. Margaret Jull Costa (London: The Harvill Press, 1999).

14. This section builds on the history of Jewish surnames sketched in Benzion C. Kaganoff, 'Jewish Surnames through the Ages: An Etymological History', *Commentary* 22:3 (1956): 249–259.

15. Kaganoff, 'Jewish Surnames through the Ages', 252.

16. The Russian Empire conducted a similar legibility project, the imposition of fixed surnames on a rural population of newly emancipated serfs in its Baltic provinces after 1816, see Andrejs Plakans and Charles Wetherell, 'Patrilines, Surnames and Family Identity', *The History of the Family* 5:2 (2000): 199–214.

17. Kaganoff, 'Jewish Surnames through the Ages', 255.

18. Kaganoff, 'Jewish Surnames through the Ages', 255 and 257.

19. Scott, *Seeing Like a State*, 78–79.

20. This means also that families are more difficult to track (both historically and in the present) than in other societies. Since Iceland has a relatively small population of 340,000 people, it was, however, possible to create a *Book of Icelanders* (*Íslendingabók*, an online database), which maps genealogical relations several centuries into the past. Recently, software engineering students from the University of Iceland have developed a smartphone app based on the *Íslendigabók*, which allows users to find out how closely related they are by 'bumping' their phones together. The 'incest prevention feature' of this app received international media attention; see, for instance, The Associated Press, 'Kissing Cousins? Icelandic App Warns You if Your Date Is a Relative', on CBC.ca, 18 April 2013, accessed 1 June 2017, http://www.cbc.ca/news/business/kissing-cousins-icelandic-app-warns-if-your-date-is-a-relative-1.1390256.

21. Cf. Barker et al., *An Atlas of English Surnames*, 11–18.

22. A. A. Fokker, 'Expressive Derivation of Proper Names in Russian', *Lingua* 9 (1961), 271.

23. Edward Stankiewicz, 'The Expression of Affection in Russian Proper Names', *The Slavic and East European Journal* 1:3 (1957), 196–210.

24. A common German nickname for Mat(t)hias is 'Matze' – some German Mat(t)hiases embrace this nickname and one German comedian uses it as his stage name, but I also have a friend who would take it as a grave insult if I ever used that name for him.

25. Simon Cole, *Suspect Identities*, 7.

26. Terry Freedman and Iseabail Macleod – in *The Wordsworth Dictionary of Surnames* (Ware: Wordsworth Reference, 1997), 1 – suggest that the transformation of village names into stable surnames coincided with the growth of big cities, since referring to the 'newcomer' by their place of origin provided the most efficient shorthand.

27. Statistiska Centralbyrån (Central Bureau of Statistics, SCB), *Bakgrundsfakta Befolknings- och välfärdsstatistik 2016:1, Personnummer* (*Background Facts, Population and Welfare Statistics 2016:1, Personal Number*), Örebro: SCB, 2016; all translations mine. This structure of the *personnummer* means that for each date of birth, there are 999 unique personal identification numbers available, 499 for women and 500 for men. SCB notes that some dates of birth – 1 January for all years in the 1980s – no longer have any available personal identification numbers, due to the influx of immigrants and refugees who often incorrectly had their dates of birth recorded as 1 January in their respective countries of origin (*Personnummer*, 14–16).

28. SCB, *Personnummer*, 5.

29. SCB, *Personnummer*, 19. It is possible, however, to restrict access to this information, or to receive a fake name and fake *personnummer* in case of a serious threat.

30. Ian Watson, 'A Short History of National Identification Numbering in Iceland', *Bifröst Journal of Social Science* 4 (2010), 81.

31. Social Security Administration, 'Identity Theft and Your Social Security Number', accessed 22 March 2017, https://www.ssa.gov/pubs/EN-05-10064.pdf.

32. The language of the bill that proposed the introduction of the *personnummer* in 1946 is quite frank in this regard. It claims that there is 'no doubt a need for an unambiguous, accessible, and easy to use tool of identification, one more transparent than [the information stored in municipal registries: name, address, date of birth, and profession]. Insofar as the committee therefore proposes the introduction of a personal number, this is just the expansion of existing systems, which, although in more limited terms, have been proven to work [such as the draft registry]' (quoted in SCB, *Personnummer*, 4).

33. Ian Watson ('A Short History of National Identification Numbering in Iceland') points out that the Icelandic *kennitala* had to evolve through several prior instantiations before it became a truly unique identifier.

34. SCB, *Personnummer*, 3 notes that 'Sweden is unique insofar as the *personnummer* has a broader use and wider acceptance than in other countries'.

35. Erika Sigvardsdotter, *Presenting the Absent: An Account of Undocumentedness in Sweden*. Dissertation, Uppsala: Kulturgeografiska institutionen, Uppsala universitet, 2012, 69–71 and 74.

36. Niklas Eklund, 'Administrative Reform in Sweden: Administrative Dualism at the Crossroad', in *Handbook of Administrative Reform: An International Perspective*, ed. Jerri Killian and Niklas Eklund (Boca Raton: CRC Press, 2008), 127–129; see also Sigvardsdotter, *Presenting the Absent*, 15.

37. Jonas F. Ludvigsson et al., 'The Swedish Personal Identity Number: Possibilities and Pitfalls in Healthcare and Medical Research', *European Journal of Epidemiology* 24 (2009), 665.

38. Ibid.

39. Skatteverket (the Swedish Tax Agency), 'Flytta till Sverige' ('Moving to Sweden'), accessed 23 March 2017, https://www.skatteverket.se/privat/folkbokforing/flyttatillsverige.4.76a43be412206334b89800018617.html.

40. SCB, *Personnummer*, 17. The *samordningsnummer* was introduced in 2000.

41. There is an ongoing housing crisis in Stockholm and other major cities in Sweden. While there is a legal requirement that landlords register with the state and while most apartments and houses for rent are owned by registered landlords and agencies, illegal subletting to short-term tenants is a widespread practice, and often the only way that those who immigrate to Sweden or come to study can find a place to live.

42. Sigvardsdotter, *Presenting the Absent*, 77; emphasis mine.

43. SCB, *Personnummer*, 5.

44. See, for instance, Katja Franko Aas, '"The Body Does Not Lie": Identity, Risk, and Trust in Technoculture', *Crime, Media, Culture* 2 (2006): 143–158; Louise Amoore, 'Biometric Borders: Governing Mobilities in the War on Terror', *Political Geography* 25 (2006): 336–351; Btihaj Ajana, 'Biometric Citizenship', *Citizenship Studies* 16:7 (2012): 851–870.

45. See for instance, David Lyon, 'The Border is Everywhere: ID Cards, Surveillance, and the Other', in *Global Surveillance and Policing*, 66–82; 'Surveillance, Security, and Social Sorting', *International Criminal Justice Review* 17:3 (2007): 161–170; 'Biometrics, Identification, and Surveillance', *Bioethics* 22:9 (2008): 499–508; and as editor: *Surveillance as Social Sorting: Privacy, Risk, and Digital Discrimination* (London and New York: Routledge, 2003).

46. Foucault adopted the imagery of the panopticon from Jeremy Bentham, who in his time proposed it as an advancement in penal reform – its point was not the actual surveillance, but the fact that the prisoners would come to *believe* that they were being watched, which is enough to discipline them; cf. Michel Foucault, *Discipline and Punish: The Birth of the Prison*, trans. Alan Sheridan, second edition (New York: Vintage Books 1995 [first translation published 1977]), 200–202.

47. I flesh out this double-character of biometry in 'Identity as Convention', 52.

48. In the wake of the refugee crisis of 2015 and 2016, the so-called Dublin III Convention, which stipulates that the first signatory state that registers an asylum-seeker is responsible for processing their application, was effectively suspended in a number of EU member states – Germany, for instance, halted all efforts to return refugees to Greece.

49. Anton Alterman, '"A Piece of Yourself": Ethical Issues in Biometric Identification', *Ethics and Information Technology* 5:3 (2003), 139–150.

50. Btihaj Ajana, 'Biometric Citizenship', 861.

51. Irma van der Ploeg, 'Written on the Body: Biometrics and Identity', *Computers and Society* 29:1 (1999), 37–44.

52. This means that complaints like David Lyon's 'Telling your story no longer suffices. It is displaying your card that counts' are plainly false; biometry has not replaced narrative, but has complemented it ('Biometrics, Identification and Surveillance', 500; cf. also Btihaj Ajana, 'Recombinant Identities', *Bioethical Inquiry* 7 (2010): 237–258).

53. This is Foucault's point in his historical study of *Polizeiwissenschaft* as the science of total administration in 'The Political Technology of Individuals'.

54. Cf. Sigvardsdotter, *Presenting the Absent*, 70–76.

55. Since 1975, genetic data from every newborn child in Sweden have been recorded in a national DNA database. Until now, this database has only been used for medical research and in rare cases, for forensic investigations.

56. Benedict Anderson, *Imagined Communities: Reflections on the Origin and Spread of Nationalism*, revised edition (London and New York: Verso Books 2006 [first published 1983]).

57. For Anderson, these 'three institutions' are central to what he calls the 'grammar of nationalism' – again with clear parallels to Scott's 'seeing like a state': 'together, they profoundly shaped the way in which the colonial state imagined its dominion – the nature of the human beings it rules, the geography of its domain, and the legitimacy of its ancestry' (*Imagined Communities*, 163–164).

58. Anderson, *Imagined Communities*, 168.

59. Anderson, *Imagined Communities*, 175.

60. Anderson, *Imagined Communities*, 175.

61. John Torpey, *The Invention of the Passport: Surveillance, Citizenship and the State* (Cambridge: Cambridge University, 2000), chs. 2 and 3.

62. Torpey, *Invention of the Passport*, 121.

63. Ruth Shipley's career and her influence on contemporary terrorist watchlists are explored in Jeffrey Kahn, *Mrs. Shipley's Ghost: The Right to Travel and Terrorist Watchlists* (Ann Arbor: The University of Michigan Press, 2013).

64. Kahn, *Mrs. Shipley's Ghost*, 35.

65. Randy Lippert, 'Governing Refugees: The Relevance of Governmentality to Understanding the International Refugee Regime', *Alternatives* 24 (1999), 300–302.

66. Thomas Rahe, 'Polnische und jüdische Displaced Persons im DP-Camp Bergen-Belsen' ('Polish and Jewish Displaced Persons in the DP Camp Bergen-Belsen'), in *Jahresbericht 2015: Schwerpunktthema Flucht, Migration, Exil*, ed. Stiftung Niedersächsische Gedenkstätten, 10–17, accessed 1 April 2017, http://www.stiftung-ng.de/fileadmin/dateien/Stiftung/Grafik_SNG/6.0.Publikationen/SNG_Jahresbericht_2015-web.pdf; see also Mark Wyman, *DPs: Europe's Displaced Persons, 1945–1951* (Ithaca and London: Cornell University Press, 1998), 131–142.

67. Scott, *Seeing Like A State*, pp. 38–46.

68. Despite the fact that terrorism poses a serious security threat to many states, the areas most affected by terrorism are those that are typically seen as its breeding ground in the West; namely countries like Iraq or Pakistan, or regions like Northern Nigeria.

69. For an analysis of the privacy risks of biometric passports, see Olli I. Heimo, Antti Hakkala and Kai K. Kimppa, 'How to Abuse Biometric Passport Systems', *Journal of Information, Communication and Ethics in Society* 10:2 (2012), 68–81.

70. The exemptions being the United Kingdom and, since early 2016, Sweden and Denmark, whose governments reintroduced systematic border controls on their land borders in the wake of the refugee crisis.

71. Emilio Parodi and Antonella Cinelli, 'Berlin Truck Attack Suspect Shot Dead by Police in Italy', *reuters.com*, 23 December 2016, accessed 1 June 2017, http://www.reuters.com/article/us-germany-truck-idUSKBN14C0JP.

72. This security loophole has become an increasingly important topic for the European security community, since the passport itself has become so secure that fraud attempts mostly focus on the application process. See for instance, Christoph Busch et al., 'Trustworthy Lifecycle Management for Public Documents: A Proposal

by the European Research Project FIDELITY in Collaboration with the EC JRC', FIDELITY homepage (2014), accessed 19 March 2017, http://www.fidelity-project.eu/media/White-Papers/FIDELITY_White-Paper_Trustworthy-lifecycle-management.pdf.

73. Cf. Matteo Ferrara, Annalisa Franco and Davide Maltoni, 'The Magic Passport', *IEEE International Joint Conference on Biometrics*, 29 September–2 October 2014, available on *IEEE Xplore*, DOI: 10.1109/BTAS.2014.6996240.

Chapter 4

Identity, Security and Trust

In the previous chapter, I set out to describe a particular 'logic' that informs our modern identity management systems and the political ambitions that shape them. In this chapter, we will take a normative look at this logic and identify its moral fault lines in more detail. I have described the main concern of contemporary identity management as a legibility issue: the modern state needs to be able to 'read' its citizens and denizens under conditions of anonymity. It cannot simply trust a person's word in verifying his or her identity; instead, it needs to construct a system of independent checks. A traveller arriving at the border, a citizen waiting in line to vote, parents reporting the birth of their newborn child: these people could in principle be *anyone*, thus the agents of the state – administrators and security forces – need to use means of identification that are not dependent on intimate knowledge.

For this purpose, modern states have developed specialized archival knowledge.[1] Personalized information about citizens and other individuals who have dealings with the state is stored in registries – previously paper based, now increasingly digital and interconnected – and the agents of the state can access this information in order to *verify* the identity of someone making a claim or requesting a service. A border guard, for instance, would check the information in the traveller's passport against his or her appearance and any other available information; in the case of the prospective voter, the clerk would check identification against an entry in a voters' registry; while another clerk would record the circumstances of a birth, verify both parents' identity and *create* a new identity for the infant – a new identity that will, under normal circumstances, become the basis of all other official identities the infant might acquire when they grow up.

This archival knowledge is *specialized* because it is suited to the needs of people who do not typically have access to intimate information about those they serve and whose identity they need to verify. It consists of selected data points that can be generalized and made legible across various contexts – consider administrative rules for how date of birth and names are to be recorded on official documents, specifications regarding passport photographs or regulations on to how to record, encrypt and store biometric information such as fingerprints.

Different tasks, of course, require different kinds of information; the border guard's process of verification is different from that of a tax office clerk. But within sovereign states, many of these systems are at least partially cross-referential. Had I – a German citizen – applied for Swedish citizenship, my tax records from my period of employment in Sweden would have been vetted through my personal number and the information tied to it – as it is one of the requirements for naturalization in Sweden that one has not cheated on one's taxes. When I was a graduate student in the United States, border guards were able to access information recorded by my university. And in Germany, most employers require a certificate of conduct issued by the Federal Ministry of Justice, which contains information about one's criminal record.

One essential feature of all archival knowledge is that it is largely decontextualized, which, as we have seen in the previous chapter and will see further, can create tension between the intimate and the official aspects of identity. The emphasis on decontextualization should not be surprising, however, since we are dealing with information that is supposed to be understood by someone who is *not familiar* with the person in front of them and their unique history and circumstances. In this, archival knowledge appears radically different from the kind of 'narrative knowledge' espoused by the narrativists discussed in chapter two. They are primarily interested in the intimate context of personal identity, thus the knowledge[2] that they see as constitutive of identity narratives springs from this context as well. The modern state, however, has to guard itself against appeals to the intimate and the personal,[3] since a centralized administration cannot function with these types of narratives – it needs to avail itself of standardized and centralized narratives. Through record-keeping, states and their institutions create histories for citizens and denizens: travel histories, employment histories and tax-payer histories. These histories may seem dry and lifeless compared to the narratives we find in intimate contexts (as well as in art), but they are no less important and their status as a narrative is no less meaningful for a moral and practical understanding of personal identity.

Administrative narrative is not just the means by which the modern state keeps track of its citizens and denizens; it is also the means by which modern citizens assert their rights and claims against the state and its agents. In this context, identification is the medium of legal personhood – and insofar as it is extremely difficult to live a decent life in a modern state without legal identification, such identification is a grounding feature of personhood. In her essay

'We Refugees' from 1943, Hannah Arendt wrote this about the condition of Jewish refugees who did not have access to legal identification:

> If we should start telling the truth that we are nothing but Jews, it would mean that we expose ourselves to the fate of human beings who, unprotected by any specific law or political convention, are nothing but human beings. I can hardly imagine an attitude more dangerous, since we actually live in a world in which human beings as such have ceased to exist for a while . . . since passports or birth certificates, and sometimes even income tax receipts, are no longer formal papers but matters of social distinction.[4]

Arendt's observation can be applied to the situation of many paperless refugees and immigrants today. In order to be recognized as a person – rather than as a mere human – by modern administrative systems, one needs to provide legal documents. Without legal identification, one runs the risk of being treated as if one did not exist, that is, as if one were a mere human animal without any social standing, but not a person. Indeed, Arendt is right that 'formal papers' are 'matters of social distinction', and I would make her claim about 'human beings as such' even stronger: there never was a time when we were human beings as such. What follows from this is a moral challenge: if legal identification confers personhood, then we need to consider the ways in which the administrative (and technological) systems that provide and maintain legal identities can fail those whom they ought to serve. The challenge is not to transcend these systems and return to some supposedly pure, pre-political and pre-technological state of humanity, nor to devise comprehensive schemes for global identity management. Rather, the challenge is to identify the gaps in our current systems and the potential for turning them against particular people and groups. This will be the main task of this chapter.

Identity management systems have two overarching goals, stemming from their internal logic of dealing with administrative knowledge. First, they aspire to be(come) closed systems – that is, entirely self- or cross-referential – and second, they aspire to reduce personal identity to a set of basic facts – that is, decontextualized data points such as the list of dates, names, places and the biometric information recorded on and stored in contemporary passports. As we shall see in what follows, these aspirations lead to both epistemic and moral conflicts, and they cannot be implemented perfectly in our messy reality.

4.1 EPISTEMIC GAPS

Ideally, identity management works by moving from basic administrative facts to more complex ones and by safeguarding more complex facts by grounding them in basic ones. The first and arguably most basic, administrative facts about my existence are the data recorded on my birth certificate. This birth certificate has served as a 'breeder document' – that is, a verification of my legal identity – for both my German ID card and my German passport. My ID card serves as legitimation when I want to vote in German municipal, state or federal elections, and I can use it to travel within the Schengen Area. My passport – in conjunction with information provided by employers or schools – has helped me obtain an American social security number and a Swedish *personnnummer*. My Swedish *personnummer*, in turn, allowed me to participate in various economic and civic activities in Sweden, such as voting in the elections to the European Parliament, or renting an apartment. So far, so good.

But many of us have probably experienced 'gaps' in such systems: for instance, in the form of clerks who cannot or do not want to fulfil a request or who find themselves unable to understand a particular piece of identification. In some American liquor stores, for instance, clerks have rejected my German passport as identification – although it contains all pertinent information in English – merely on account of it being a foreign identification document (consider in this context that it is easier to obtain or forge an American driver's licence than to obtain or forge a EU passport). In Sweden, you need both valid identification and a valid *personnummer* to open a bank account; and I was told that some banks reject even EU passports and insist on identification issued by Swedish authorities in addition to the *personnummer*.

The gaps in identity management systems – miscommunication, failed transfers of information, lack of 'readable' information – point to the fact that these systems are in actuality neither closed nor perfectly cross-referential. We can illustrate this by adapting two well-known schools of analytic epistemology to the issue: foundationalism and coherentism. The basic question of all epistemology is how we can ever come to be justified in calling something *knowledge*. The classic definition of knowledge, accepted by virtually all Western philosophy until Edmund Gettier upended it with a three-page-paper in 1963, was 'justified, true belief'.[5] For our purposes here – how do we know whether someone's identity claims are valid? – both the term 'justified' and the term 'true' pose philosophical challenges.

Within the narrative account of identity that I have defended in chapter two, the truth of identity claims cannot be rooted in biological or psychological facts – it must instead be rooted in records or the social recognition of personal identity. As I have argued, 'recognition' should be understood in a very broad sense; it can encompass intimate relationships as well as administrative processes. Now, if the truth of identity claims consists in recognition, then we face a serious epistemic challenge: even if we allow that recognition can be a social fact, how can another ever be *justified* in assessing facts of recognition? In other words, how can a third person ever observe my recognition of another person? The problem is that even if recognition is socially real and morally relevant, it would seem that the 'facts' of recognition are vague, flexible and impervious to independent confirmation – thus very poor candidates for ever constituting any kind of *knowledge*. However, the moral and political conflicts that emerge around these issues are real and must be taken seriously.

In the previous chapter, we saw how modern bureaucracies attempted to deal with this problem. Cartographers turned the messy reality of traditional rural land use into neat cadastral records and maps; city planners tried to impose transcendental order on narrow and unruly neighbourhoods; administrators perfected record-keeping and the use of identity documents to make persons 'legible' for the state. As an administrative effort in nation-building, this undertaking was efficient and ingenious. But epistemically, it remained necessarily incomplete. Let us see why this is so.

The ideal of modern identity management is foundationalist: foundationalists believe that all knowledge – all *justification* of true beliefs[6] – can be derived from basic facts and basic knowledge of these facts. In administrative terms: any interaction based on identity verification should in principle be justifiable in terms of identity documents and other pieces of evidence that are themselves grounded in basic breeder documents. This is the ideal that undergirds the interconnectedness and interoperability of different identity records sketched earlier: I receive an identity card if I can produce a birth certificate, a passport if I can produce an identity card and administrative recognition in foreign countries if I can produce a valid passport. The 'basic fact' in this scheme is the birth certificate and whatever electronic records of my person may be linked to it. Other identity documents and new records then form a structure of more complex identity facts. But in principle, this structure is rooted in that first administrative act of creating a new legal identity. Now, it is clear that both record-keeping and compliance with administrative demands would need to be *perfect* for any actual system to approach this ideal. However, record-keeping is messy and often incomplete, identity management systems typically have a hard time communicating across international borders, and people do not always comply. So administrative systems have to find ways to work around such gaps in order to remain functional. That is to say, these systems need to have provisions for what happens when someone cannot provide the desired identity document, or when the records that exist of them are incomplete.

For this reason, actual identity management systems are typically open to evidence and testimony from other 'systems' and adjust their standards to their own incompleteness. This requires what we might describe as a coherentist epistemic attitude. Coherentism is foundationalism's philosophical rival; coherentists contend that rather than grounding the justification of knowledge in basic known facts, it is to be assessed it in terms of how well it fits with the existing network of facts and beliefs around us.[7] Consider, for instance, how you might approach hearing something on the news that confuses you and which you think cannot be true – for instance, that a beloved television personality has been accused of sexually assaulting children, or that a dictator who has ruled with the proverbial iron fist for decades loses in a democratic election and decides to step down.[8] Your first instinct would likely be to compare it with everything else you know about the country or the person in question. You would wonder how well the news fitted with what you thought you knew, rather than trying to reduce it to some basic facts about the matter. Indeed, the latter might be impossible, since you are unlikely to have direct access to eyewitnesses, police reports and the like.[9] Coherentism has the obvious disadvantage that it seems to allow that belief networks can attain the status of knowledge simply in virtue of how well the beliefs in these networks cohere – for instance, someone who believes that a cabal of very rich and very powerful men secretly runs the world might have a very coherent belief system in the sense that they would only accept new information that fitted with their initial conspiracy theory and dismiss everything else. But quite obviously, their belief system as a whole lacks justification, precisely because it is so selective and ignores so much. In the field of epistemology, some coherentists have tried to meet this objection by privileging some observational and experiential beliefs, creating a blend of foundationalist and coherentist justificatory strategies that is sometimes described as 'weak foundationalism'.[10] I would suggest that weak foundationalism is also an apt description of administrative systems that blend foundationalist and coherentist attitudes – and perhaps even of the way in which most of us approach questions of belief, justification and truth in everyday life.

But when and why does identity management adopt coherentist structures? Here is another anecdote from my time in the United States: a close friend in Boston moved house and in the process accidentally threw away his birth certificate. Around the same time, a suburban cop, who liked neither my friend's looks nor his untidy car, decided to emphasize the fact that his driver's licence was no longer valid by cutting it to pieces. This meant that my friend no longer had the two identity documents that could prove his legal personhood – the birth certificate being the breeder document and the driver's licence being the most commonly used general identification across the United States. This also meant that we could only ever go out to one bar, where he would not get carded because the staff knew him personally. Now according to the foundationalist logic sketched earlier in the text, my friend should have been in danger of losing his identity, since he was without the two basic identification documents upon which his legal identity rested. He could, however, still apply for a U.S. passport – and did so, after a considerable amount of complaining from us about only ever going to that one bar with him. This process required that he appear in a U.S. post office with two American citizens with valid identification who could bear witness to his identity. In my friend's case, we could say that the foundationalist ideal was suspended in favour of integrating knowledge from another system of knowledge – in this case, personal testimony. This integration hinged on the coherence of the witnesses' testimony with my friends' testimony – this made it possible to re-establish the 'basic facts' of my friend's legal identity with testimonial support.

We find similar coherentist approaches in refugee status determinations and in the legal administration of gender changes. In the case of refugee status determinations, administrators and lawyers need to establish – among other things – whether the asylum-seeker's claims about the persecution they endured, and the lack of state protection from it, are credible. This cannot be done in terms of basic facts about either the asylum-seeker or their country of origin alone. Rather, it involves a careful weighing of the particular claims made by the asylum-seeker, their general trustworthiness, general knowledge about the country and specific knowledge about the part of the country the applicant claims to be from. This task is even more difficult when the asylum-seeker has no identity documents – in this case, administrators and lawyers also need to establish the credibility of their claims about their nationality.

This careful weighing of different kinds of evidence can, of course, go wrong, both epistemically and morally – and it can be used against the asylum-seeker. This is often the case where applicants seek protection from a category of persecution that is particularly hard to prove – for instance, the persecution of gay and queer minorities.[11] There is emerging literature on this topic that shows that even administrators and lawyers in generally gay-friendly countries tend to use prejudicial or outdated information about gay and queer persons and their situation in the country. It has been reported, for instance, that Australia used information from gay travel guides for Western tourists to conclude that countries like Morocco did not persecute their gay citizens.[12] German courts have sometimes rejected asylum applications on the grounds that gay asylum-seekers should just move to a different part of their country or that they should be 'discreet' about their sexuality, even in countries where homosexuality is punished with long prison sentences or death.[13]

Refugee status determinations, especially for gay applicants, are administrative and legal processes that depend heavily on contextual knowledge: when claims are evaluated, the asylum-seeker's narrative – whether their story is coherent and believable, what impression they make on the court and the administrators – is as important or even more important than particular facts of their case, especially since such facts might be elusive.

In the case of legal gender changes, the coherentist attitude is even more pronounced. A legal gender change implies a change of basic administrative facts on some or all of a person's identity documents. This could be their driver's licence, their passport and in some cases their birth certificate. Unsurprisingly, allowing people to change the gender on their birth certificate tends to be among the most contested rights claims advanced by the trans community – and it is also the one with the strongest coherentist bent. Foundationalist common sense would have it that the birth certificate should reflect the biological sex of the child at birth, as perceived and assigned by a medical professional. Allowing a trans person to change this entry would not only cast doubt on medical authority but also undermine the very foundation of record-keeping, since it revises one of the first building blocks of a legal identity – since information about a newborn's sex is typically treated as indispensable by the authorities. Paisley Currah and Lisa Jean Moore have chronicled the legal struggles to allow changes of the sex recorded on birth certificates in New York City, and they suggest that one attitude that has remained constant among opponents of more liberal policies since the 1960s is fear of fraudulent abuse and the notion that the legal category of sex must refer to *permanent* features.[14] In the earliest legal challenge discussed by Currah and Moore, the courts insisted that the biological 'truth' of a body could never be altered, not even by surgery; while in more recent discussions, evidence of surgery and hormonal treatment was demanded as support for the required permanence of the desired legal sex change.[15] So even where lawmakers are willing to allow sex changes on legal documents, they want independent assurances that these changes reflect an enduring truth about the applicant. Such assurances form a sort of coherentist safety net around the foundationalist 'truth' of the sex assignment at birth that is being challenged in these processes. But how this safety net is designed legally and administratively varies dramatically from country to country, and sometimes even within countries.

In the United States, most states by now allow changes to the sex designated on the birth certificate; some (Kansas, Ohio and Idaho), however, do not issue new birth certificates with a changed sex; and one state (Tennessee) has a statutory prohibition of sex changes on birth certificates.[16] Internationally, many countries now allow legal sex changes, but virtually all of them insist on independent confirmation of the applicants' claims – in the form of an official diagnosis of gender identity disorder or gender dysphoria or evidence of hormonal and surgical treatment. Argentina, Malta and Denmark currently have the most progressive trans legislations in the world and are the only countries that effectively allow trans persons to self-determine their legal sex.[17] Until Denmark changed its transgender law in 2014, however, it required persons who wished to change their legal sex to be surgically sterilized; and whether the progressive changes towards self-declaration in these three countries will trigger more widespread change remains to be seen. The point here is that the ruling paradigm in legislations that do recognize legal sex changes is *not* to allow such changes based on the applicant's testimony alone.

4.2 TRUSTWORTHY IDENTIFICATION

What general lesson can we draw from these examples? I think the most important lesson – morally and epistemically – is that contemporary identity administration cannot be a closed system. It is, of course, *theoretically* possible to conceive of such a system, and some philosophers have suggested that it would also be *practically* desirable. In their paper 'Body, Biometrics, and Identity', Emilio Mordini and Sonia Massari argue that biometric identity management need not be a Leviathan – an all-powerful surveillance machine – but could instead enhance individual autonomy and legal security.[18] As I argued in relation to the Nordic *personnummer*, such a system certainly has the *potential* to work for individuals and in their interest; but under current circumstances, it is likely to create groups of outsiders who cannot participate in it. Mordini and Massari envision a benevolent identity management supersystem; yet such a system could only work in everyone's interest under two conditions: one, that there is a binding, efficacious and truly global agreement on how to handle identity management; and, two, that everyone has easy access to state-of-the-art identity management technologies. Their idealistic viewpoint calls for nothing short of a global revolution of identity management, which would require massive investment and political goodwill.

We are currently far away from fulfilling either of the conditions I just named. Politically and administratively, identity management remains one of the least harmonized fields of administration across international boundaries and even across many regional and local boundaries. As we saw in the previous chapter, while the biometric EU-passport does conform to international standards, birth certificates across the European Union do not, which creates a security loophole: someone might apply for a genuine biometric passport with a birth certificate whose validity cannot be ascertained by clerks not trained in a foreign bureaucracy and a foreign language or script. Financially, many countries and individuals cannot afford state-of-the-art technologies; there might be no facilities to mass-produce biometric passports, or where they can be produced, they might be prohibitively expensive for the majority of the population.[19] Even in so-called developed countries, the cost of acquiring a machine-readable, biometric passport – by now the *only* choice of passport – can be significant: in the United Kingdom, the fees for a standard passport rose from £5 in 1975 to £77.50 in 2009 (and have since fallen to £72.50).

Now, if we admit that identity management has to work in imperfect conditions, then we must also ask how its moral and epistemic challenges can be addressed fairly and equitably in light of issues such as unequal access to specific technologies and inevitable gaps and inconsistencies in record-keeping. And it would be impractical to apply an 'ideal' standard of identity management and verification to the 'non-ideal' status quo of our bureaucracies. Yet this is what many political and technological solutions seek to do: they formulate solutions for ideal circumstances, not for our non-ideal reality.

In December 2015, I spoke at a European research project conference in Brussels, presenting some thoughts about trust in the border control context to a mixed audience of computer engineers, policy-makers, administrators and police officers. What struck me most about the feedback I received was that border police representatives seemed to agree most with my diagnosis and thought that I had expressed a concern that they had long had with the way policy-makers and engineers view and regulate their work. In addition to general concerns about cost-cutting and increasing workloads, they expressed worries about how technological advances affect their jobs. In my talk, I had suggested that in contemporary, state-of-the-art border security systems, there are at least three different kinds of trust at play: epistemic trust, social trust and trust in technology. Not only are these different kinds of trust, they can clash with one another. Let me spell out this concern with a concrete example. Suppose you are working as a border guard at the airport of a major European city. The airport serves a large number of passengers who have to pass immigration checks. In order to ease the workload for individual border guards, the airport has installed automated passport readers. These readers can read information off the passport and scan passengers' faces, matching the two. Ostensibly, automated passport readers ease the border guards' workload and shorten queues; yet they still require human oversight, and so there will always be a border guard present who needs to assess whether, for instance, someone who holds up the queue at an automated scanner and seems nervous is simply struggling to use the technology or whether they are trying to cheat the machine. Even in regular, in-person border checks, border guards are often presented with additional information, which they need to process while they inspect the passport. As I have already mentioned, U.S. border guards would also see information coming from, for instance, an exchange student's school, or from the employer of a foreign worker.

Plans for future automated systems take this integration of electronically generated data even further. The European Union, for instance, is planning a European Passenger Name Record (PNR), which could be exchanged between and data-mined by national border police for information such as travel histories or even meal choices on flights.[20] Such information might then also appear – in the form of alerts – on the terminals of individual border guards, who could be informed that an individual traveller poses a risk and should be questioned more thoroughly. In the United States, systems are under development that can remotely take biometric readings from the passenger – such as their eye movement or heart rate – and test their reaction to basic immigration-related questions that border guards select in advance. Such systems, if implemented, would amount to a 'lie detector' test at the border – but this does not necessarily make the task of the border guards who attend to the system any easier.[21] Traditionally, a border guard needs to know the correct formats for international travel documents – so that they can quickly recognize fake IDs – and they need to be able to spot behavioural clues that might suggest criminal intent. With the expanding role of information technologies, border guards also need to assess the validity of any additional information they might receive during a border check – and given that an average border check lasts between eight and ten seconds, this is not an easy task.

For an engineer, creating an innovative border control system might well represent a crowning achievement of their skill; and policy-makers will enjoy hearing about how much such a system would reduce both the human workload of border police and the reliability of immigration checks. In terms of trust – 'trustworthy identification' being a buzzword in the security community – such a system may well look as if it is combining the best of digital efficiency and human experience, thus seem particularly reliable. But we must consider that the trust, experience and knowledge in question are not cumulative – they cannot simply be added together. Consider, first, how a border guard typically works in an in-person situation: They check the passengers' documents, matching the photograph to the passenger's face, checking whether all documents are valid and bear the same name, looking for clues as to whether the documents might be forged. The border guard makes an assessment of possible problem cases in light of the administrative information available to them and then in light of the demeanour of the actual passenger. This type of assessment requires *epistemic trust*: In each individual assessment, there must be a cut-off point where the border guard decides that they now have enough information to either let the passenger through or take them aside for further questioning. Epistemic trust in this case means trust in the sources of their information, such as trust that a valid document was issued by an authorized agency, and that it has not been obtained fraudulently. However, the physical presence of the traveller complicates things. Human beings can be very quick to make judgements about another's intentions and attitudes. These judgements – like any human judgement – can be influenced by conscious or unconscious biases. A person's manner of speech, their appearance or their gender can result in them being seen as uneducated or incompetent.[22] A border guard needs to make a judgement about another's intentions in less than ten seconds. Even if they try their best not to be influenced by bias, their experience alone will likely provide them with hunches as to who is suspicious and who is not. These hunches may well be for the most part correct and an appropriate reflection of their work experience. However, they are not of the same kind as the epistemic trust that informs the check of the documents in front of them.

Hunches are instances of *social trust* or social mistrust. Social trust tracks our familiarity with things and persons. If we find ourselves in surroundings that seem familiar, we are more likely to trust people; and if we surround ourselves with people who are – in some respect – like us, we are more likely to perceive our surroundings as friendly. Of course, a perception of familiarity or lack thereof can be misplaced; thus, there is a risk that social (mis)trust undermines an otherwise epistemically warranted judgement.[23] Our border guard might probe someone less thoroughly or more thoroughly in light of how familiar the person seems, which, in turn, can skew their epistemic judgement about the traveller's documents.

The issue is further complicated by the involvement of additional digitally processed data. An automated border control kiosk can provide a human border guard with useful information, which the guard could not obtain in the mere seconds they spend with each traveller. But the provision of this additional information could also lead to information overload, thus undermine judgements that might otherwise be reliable. Take as an example the process matching of passport photos to actual faces and of encrypted biometric data on the passport to live fingerprints, which automated border control gates can standardly deliver. The matches created in these cases are never identical matches – rather, they map probabilities: if the live fingerprint matches or the live facial image correlates to the data stored on the passport with a high enough probability, both traveller and attending border guard would get a green light. However, neither traveller nor guard would have insight into the process itself and the exact probabilities – all the guard needs to know is that the match is 'good enough' in order not to interfere in the process – nor would a guard be able to know exactly why a traveller received a red light. The border guard in charge of observing the queue for the automated border control would not be able to distinguish glitches in the system from someone who has trouble adjusting their face or fingers to the machine,[24] or from someone who is actually trying to trick the system. Where border control processes are supported by electronic systems, the human end users typically do *not* have insight into how these systems work.

The problem is compounded in anticipated systems that might provide a risk score for travellers based on additional information, such as the PNR scenario I briefly sketched earlier in the text. While such systems raise serious privacy concerns, they are on track to being installed.[25] Now suppose that a border guard receives an alert from such a complex system, but has no insight into how it was obtained. What are they to do with such information – especially in circumstances where the risk does not match their own impression of the traveller and their check of the relevant documents? Should they treat the hint given by the electronic system as reliable? Border guards are by law the ultimate arbiters on whether someone gets access to a state's territory or not, and electronic support is supposed to be no more than support; but its presence places an additional epistemic burden on the border guard.

One aspect of this problem is that electronic systems of this kind are usually not built to be transparent to those who directly work with the results they generate. This makes *e-trust* necessary – in the sense that an administrative agent needs to trust that an electronic system is *generally* reliable, despite not being able to assess the validity of each individual result. It should become clearer at this point how the different kinds of trust that are at play here clash with one another. We have, first, epistemic trust: a cut-off point for an in-person assessment of identity documents and identity claims. Second, we have social trust: the way in which perceived similarities and dissimilarities can skew epistemic judgements in one direction or another. Third, we have e-trust: judgements or assumptions about the reliability of electronic systems. As we have seen, social trust and mistrust can undercut epistemic trust in documents, insofar as they can make a valid identity claim seem questionable, or an invalid claim believable. A similar tension can occur between epistemic trust and e-trust, especially where electronic systems are not transparent to their end users. It is not necessarily the case that electronic systems improve judgements made by individual humans. Sometimes, they might undermine sound individual judgements and at others, individual administrative agents might simply disregard electronic advice, because they cannot understand how it was formed: a 'red light' might be ignored because the person in question seems trustworthy and their documents do not show any inconsistencies. In other contexts, where individual human agents are asked to trust the workings of a machine, they might refrain from taking individual epistemic responsibility, delegating it all to a system they do not understand. So what at first glance seems like a combination of two kinds of trust may well turn out to be the replacement of one with another.

Furthermore, social trust can collide with e-trust to undermine the reliability of electronic systems. Systems like the one sketched earlier in the text – based on specific algorithms – need to be 'trained', that is, their algorithms need to tested and fine-tuned with input from humans who have actual experience with the relevant tasks – in our case, police, border guards and other security specialists. So there is always a risk that any biases that these human experts might have will be reproduced by the electronic system. As a result, the system would not provide support but merely reproduce existing biases.[26] Among engineers and security experts, these kinds of concern may well be countered by supposing that if we could just make these systems better, the problem would disappear. But the issue here is not merely inbuilt bias. The issue is that we inevitably have to build such systems from incomplete knowledge, and that they will inevitably have to deal with imperfect end users. Assuming that a system would work perfectly if constructed in perfect conditions does not help but rather exacerbates the problem. Yet I am not suggesting that identity management *as a whole* is flawed, or that it is a pointless undertaking. Rather, I emphasize the issue of trust, because it points to the relevant moral risks – and without a careful appraisal of those risks, we cannot improve the ways we handle official identities and matters of border security.

In what follows, I will focus on what I take to be a particularly dangerous way of handling these matters, namely to replace the identification of individual identities with the stigmatization of group identities. In order to understand why this is so dangerous, and how it connects to individual identities, we need first to consider what makes group identities vulnerable – and indeed, breeding grounds for hate and violence.

4.3 HYPOCHONDRIAC IDENTITIES

In her book, *Gegen den Hass (Against Hate)*,[27] German publicist Carolin Emcke attempts to understand how nationalist hate could have returned with such force, both in Germany and other countries.[28] Like me, Emcke sees important connections between hate directed at immigrants and refugees and hate directed at women and queer minorities.

> If there is one thing which the dogmatism of the fanatics depends on, it is unambiguousness. They need a pure doctrine of a 'homogeneous' nation, a 'true' religion, a 'primordial' tradition, a 'natural' family and an 'authentic' culture.[29]

This dogmatism must simplify, it must understand the world in mutually exclusive terms of friends and enemies, good and evil, and it elevates purity to the status of a political and social virtue. The obsession with purity also helps us understand the role that the construction of group identities plays in this return of nationalist, anti-feminist and anti-queer hate.[30] Emcke notes that many propagandists who clamour for the return to a 'pure' nation appear to think in pseudo-biological terms.[31] In their imagination, the nation and its civil society are a body that needs to be protected against external influences threatening to contaminate it. It is no coincidence that the German term *Volks-körper* (literally: ethnic body) was prominently used in Nazi propaganda and that the Nazis often portrayed their enemies as diseases or pests that threatened the *Volkskörper*'s health. The infamous pseudo-documentary *Der ewige Jude* (*The Eternal Jew*, from 1940) presented images of Jews living in crowded and unsanitary conditions in ghettos or concentration camps as if they had chosen these conditions themselves, and likened the migration of Eastern European Jews to the migration of rats. Today, we are witnessing a return to such vile metaphors; in February 2017, Sachsen-Anhalt's member of parliament and chair of the far-right *Alternative für Deutschland*'s (AfD) parliamentary group, André Poggenburg, described leftist protesters who had disrupted an AfD-sponsored event as 'a tumor growing on the national body'.[32] Emcke writes:

> This biologization of political speech (and of political imagination) supports and attaches itself to notions of hygiene, which are transposed from the context of health care for human bodies to [political care] for a society: thus cultural or religious diversity appears as if it threatened the national health of the *Volkskörper*.[33]

This way of thinking about nation and society is indicative of a 'strangely hypochondriac identity'.[34] Any kind of difference – whether cultural, religious or sexual – becomes an existential threat to the nation's integrity, precisely because this integrity is defined through its – cultural, religious or sexual – purity. Hypochondriac thinking is especially prominent among those who vehemently and sometimes violently reject 'multiculturalism', 'gender ideology' or an alleged 'gay agenda' – cultural and social changes that are perceived as an existential threat.[35] The political hypochondriac relates to any kind of change or ambiguity as the medical hypochondriac relates to minor pains and inconveniences – worrying that they might be the signs of a life-threatening illness. Let us consider two examples of 'hypochondriac identity' at work in politics, one from the United States, one from Germany. The first is President Trump's initial executive order restricting immigration in January 2017 – the so-called Muslim ban. The second is the ongoing policy debate about sexual education in schools in Germany.[36]

At the time of writing, Trump's executive order – which, among other things, banned entry form seven Muslim-majority countries and permanently suspended the Syrian refugee resettlement programme – sparked global protest. It has been contested in court and regarded as a shoddily drafted text, and it has created confusion as to how it was supposed to be implemented – both with the Department of Homeland Security (DHS) and Immigration and Customs Enforcement (ICE) and with foreign governments, who did not know how to advise citizens holding dual citizenship.[37]

As many commentators – particularly on social media – pointed out, the Muslim ban affected some countries whose nationals had not committed any acts of terror in the United States, and it left out two countries where the largest groups among terrorist infiltrators who committed attacks on American soil in the last forty-one years originated: Saudi-Arabia and Pakistan.[38] Just to remind ourselves: fifteen of the terrorists found directly responsible for the 9/11 attacks were Saudi nationals. Moreover, the ban completely halted refugee and resettlement programmes that already have some of the strictest vetting processes in the world.[39]

While Trump and his administration claimed that their purpose is to 'keep America safe', critics have pointed out that it is unclear how the ban would achieve this aim. Whether Trump himself understood the language of the document he signed and whether he honestly believed that the ban would increase security are questions I cannot answer. But what his language and that of his supporters suggests – especially in response to the first court orders that halted the ban's implementation – is that factual, measurable security was of secondary importance. The ban did not address an outside threat. Its target audience was a nation that had been made to *feel* as if such a threat, of existential proportions, was lingering outside its borders. And the natural response to a *perceived* threat is aggressive measures that increase *perceived* security. Summarily put: the target of the ban was not international terrorism. The target was a collective hypochondriac: a nation willing to believe that it was being overrun by immigrants, Muslims and criminals, who were, in turn, aided in their nefarious schemes by liberals, feminists and queers with their agenda of 'political correctness'. Trump's campaign motto 'Make America Great Again' and the revival of the fascist and isolationist 'America First' slogan in his inauguration speech played to exactly the same sentiment. Whether or not the United States was actually struggling socially and economically was at most of secondary importance. What mattered was that enough people *felt* as if things were taking an apocalyptic turn.

Although it deals at first glance with an entirely different matter, the German debates about reforming sexual education in schools are indicative of a structurally similar sentiment. In several federal states – Niedersachsen and Baden-Württemberg among them – left-liberal governments planned to make 'sexual diversity' part of the school curriculum by age-appropriately informing pupils about homosexuality and variants of sexual identity such as intersex. Opponents of these plans, coming mostly from the churches, groups of concerned parents and conservative and far right parties, attacked these plans as *Frühsexualisierung* (literally: premature sexualization).[40] In this case, mere information about the fact that there is more to sexuality than heterosexual coitus and procreation was perceived as an existential threat to the children's development and often ascribed to a sinister 'gay lobby'. What is particularly interesting is that so many of the arguments advanced against the reform portrayed heterosexuality – and by extension the traditional family and marriage – as fragile institutions on the verge of collapse: simply talking about the existence of queer behaviours and gay identities was seen as too much for heterosexual norms to bear.[41]

The national and heterosexual identities that are being constructed in these discourses are hypochondriac insofar as their essence lies in their fragility and their extreme vulnerability to outside threats: the United States must defend itself against terrorist infiltrators; parents and churches must protect their children from too much information about human sexuality. In the case of Trump's rhetoric and the rhetoric of the shrillest voices in the German debates, these threats are made out to be *catastrophic*. It is not simply that one *disagrees* with progressive changes to school curricula or with generous refugee policies – rather, such policies are portrayed as aggressive, potentially violent acts. They are seen elements of a 'culture war', in which there is no compromise.[42]

4.4 THE MISTRUST LOOP

So far, I have talked about the role of trust in identification management and verification and about the recent surge in nationalist rhetoric around what I call a hypochondriac identity. The next step is to connect these two elements and to show how they are exploited for political purposes. Let us return for a moment to the basic question we considered in the previous chapter: *Why do states engage in identity management?* My proposal was that official identities are a decontextualized analogue of the intimate knowledge that can develop only in close-knit communities. What intimate knowledge is for families or friends, official identities and practices of identity verification are for the state. Since the state cannot know and trust its citizens in the same way that intimates know and trust one another, we should expect the relevant practices of 'knowing' and 'trusting' to be different. Record-keeping, on this view, is just another form of generating knowledge for the sake of trust, analogous perhaps to the way close friends indulge in memories of their relationship. But we need to keep in mind what I have said about different types of trust: not all trust – whether between intimates, or between citizens and the state – is grounded in knowledge: not all trust is epistemic trust. This makes social trust relevant for identification processes, and as we have seen, social trust can come into conflict with epistemic trust (and e-trust). So there may be quite different reasons why states engage in identity management. Indeed, governments might not *want to trust* their citizens and residents, but want rather *to foster mistrust* in order to further their particular political goals. The same administrative machinery that can be mobilized for quick and reliable identification in the pursuit of benign ends can easily be turned against specific groups.

On this matter, it is illuminating to consider Niklas Luhmann's view of trust. He is not interested in trust as an individual emotional or epistemic attitude, but rather seeks to analyse its social function. This function, according to him, is the 'reduction of complexity'.[43] Trust in this sense is a necessity of everyday life,[44] yet we rarely think about it: I trust that the mail I send to my colleagues will be delivered to them and only to them. I trust that doctors are giving me largely sound medical advice. I trust that respectable news sources provide me with mostly accurate news. I trust that the food I buy in the supermarket is not poisonous. This sort of trust operates in the background of our everyday agency, and only if it breaks down, do we give it any thought. Such breakdowns of trust are particularly interesting for my purposes here. Sometimes, trust can be withheld or withdrawn for good reasons: when considering major surgery, for instance, it would generally seem a good idea to get a second opinion from another surgeon. When you want to account for potential political biases in your favourite news sources, it would seem apt to broaden your media consumption, and, say, read at least one conservative newspaper in addition to the liberal and leftist papers to which have subscribed (and vice versa). Such hesitation is informed by reasonable doubt, poses no particular epistemic or moral challenge and does not undermine the social function of trust. Doubt can, however, become unreasonable where it is no longer informed by a selective need for additional information but by a totalizing mistrust against entire institutions. Totalizing mistrust grows quickest in environments that are shielded from epistemic challenges but rife with affective appeals. Donald Trump's presidential campaign systematically evoked this kind of mistrust, as does anti-vaccination rhetoric, or campaigns against processed foods, or complaints about 'the mainstream media' or 'political correctness'. All of these are driven by *emotions* directed against entire institutions or groups of people: the feeling that all politicians are crooks; that all doctors are in the pocket of the pharma industry; that any ingredient in foodstuffs whose name you cannot pronounce is 'chemical' and therefore poisonous;[45] that all asylum-seekers are potential terrorists. To be clear: I do not believe that trust and mistrust can be entirely rational, nor that they should be. Trust and mistrust in their manifold social manifestations will always have an emotional component – be that a willingness to believe that most other people have fundamentally good intentions, or a certain background wariness about life and society. The point here is to distinguish (mis)trust that is at least receptive to new experiences ('I might change my views about refugees if I got to know some of them personally') from (mis) trust that is entirely solipsistic ('Nothing could ever change my views about refugees; I just *know* that they are all bad people').

It is tempting to think that people driven by totalizing mistrust simply lack trust. But even someone who trusts neither established institutions, nor people with expertise and authority needs to get information and advice. Consider a parent who is afraid of vaccines and perhaps of 'modern medicine' generally: if their mistrust were simply lack of trust – that is, if they genuinely believed that they could not trust *anyone* – where would they go with their sick child? Luhmann thinks that it is a practical impossibility not to trust at all: trust makes the complexity of life bearable. It allows us to avoid or significantly shorten decision processes that might otherwise take a lot of time and require expertise we do not have ourselves. In this sense, the social function of trust is analogous to the demanded fulfilled by search engines and websites that allow you to compare the prices of different companies for flights or hotels: instead of checking many single items, one after another, the website gives you a neat little ranking of options. Just like the social function of trust allows you to *assume* that medical doctors, trained carpenters or airline pilots are competent without needing to check their individual backgrounds, a search engine or price comparison website allows you to treat its cumulative results as authoritative without needing to check the listings for each individual provider of the service you need.[46] Even the mistrustful person is going to have a need for the kind of background stability to social life that trust provides. So their mistrust needs to serve some function that is analogous to the social function of trust: mistrust as a purely sceptical attitude is unsustainable.

Luhmann notes, with some impatience: 'Even someone whom the world makes nauseous and afraid must take his heart medication, pay his taxes, brush his teeth, have his car checked out by a mechanic, and thus engage with the world.'[47] Of course, some people do *not* take their medication, do *not* pay their taxes and refuse to engage with the world. Yet this refusal typically does not amount to mistrust of *everything* – rather, it is a matter of very selective trust. People who are sceptical of vaccines often follow the advice of charlatans. People who think that 'the media' lie to them often get their information from filter bubbles and share and repeat lies and bullshit without a second thought. Those who try to avoid paying taxes to the state might throw their money into an extreme libertarian lifestyle and become victims of fraud.[48] Social life is not possible without trust; and like everyone else, despite their mistrust, these people need to trust in *something* or *someone*. This is why Luhmann says that mistrust 'is not just the opposite of trust, but as such also its functional equivalent'.[49]

Someone who trusts in personal, social or institutional arrangements makes their life *simpler*: If I trust my friends to pay back the money I lent them, or trust the postal service to deliver my mail, I have fewer things to worry about and more time and energy for other things. Even mistrustful people need to make their life simpler in this way. But where the need to trust and a totalizing mistrust coincide, charlatans, fraudsters and demagogues have an opportunity to manipulate people. There are many contemporary examples of this, especially on social media, where discussion of political and social issues is often dominated by resentment and misinformation. Many of those who voted for Donald Trump in the 2016 presidential election in the United States regarded Hillary Clinton as a corrupt establishment candidate – and decided to trust a reality television 'star' and con artist. Many of those in the United Kingdom who voted for Brexit in the summer of 2016 regarded the European Union as deeply untrustworthy but were willing to trust Nigel Farage and Boris Johnson, both of whom merrily lied for their political cause. Many who post on behalf of extremist groups and parties seem impervious to factual arguments when challenged. Suppose someone claims that immigrants and refugees are responsible for increasing crime rates; and suppose someone else challenges this claim by posting a statistic showing either that crime rates have not risen or that immigrants and refugees are not responsible for increasing crime rates. What happens? It is *unlikely* that the original poster would simply retract their statements and change their views; rather, it is likely that they would instead claim that the statistical data had been manipulated. The same attitude is apparent in the resurgence of the German term *Lügenpresse*, not just in Germany but also in abroad. Literally 'lying press', *Lügenpresse* is a propaganda term coined by Goebbels to denounce the free press of the Weimar Republic. In the German Federal Republic, the term resurfaced in the wake of the refugee crisis of 2015 and 2016: protesters in the PEGIDA[50] marches chanted 'Lü-gen-pres-se' to express their complete distrust of anything the media reported, and among those who sympathize with PEGIDA or the *Alternative für Deutschland*, there was a sense that the media deliberately covered up problems concerning 'criminal refugees'.[51]

What is particularly interesting here is that this extreme mistrust does not actually seem to translate into a broader consumption of media outlets in the sense that someone who is concerned about ideological bias in the press would make an effort to read newspapers opposed to their own views. Rather, it seems that those who honestly believe that 'the media' are actually *lying* to them retreat into their own filter bubbles where their mistrust is amplified, receiving positive feedback from like-minded others[52] and where, consequently, falsehoods can spread unchallenged. So those who are prone to totalizing mistrust actually seem *more* vulnerable to misinformation, propaganda and lies. Luhmann describes this apparent paradox as follows:

> In order to define any sort of practically sensible situation, the mistrustful person requires functionally equivalent strategies for the reduction of complexity. He needs to expect the worst.... The mistrustful person needs more information and yet narrows down the pool of information sources that he can rely on. He becomes *more* dependent on *less* information.[53]

Faced with a complex and confusing world, the mistrustful person turns to simple, linear explanations – explanations which tend to be misleading or plainly false.

Now, what does the example of totalizing mistrust have to do with the state's involvement in identity management? I propose to think of some state agency as analogous to the agency of mistrustful persons. This analogy could arise either as a result of systemic flaws and gaps in legal and administrative systems, or on account of a specific political agenda. As an example of the first kind, we might cite over-reliance on technical solutions for security problems, as discussed earlier. As an example of the second kind, we might consider the rhetoric and the actions of tyrants and autocrats who blame the problems of the state and its citizens on particular groups that are coded as 'foreign'. Examples of this second strategy include Trump's Muslim ban, or propaganda in Russia and Uganda that condemns homosexuality as a 'Western import' and a threat to the moral fabric of the nation, thus excluding gays and lesbians from membership in the national community. What is the purpose of such propaganda? The explicit purpose of the Muslim ban was to 'keep America safe'. We have already debunked this claim. Its actual purpose was to address vague fears in the population that consider all Muslims – even American citizens – as a potential danger and suggest that they cannot be full citizens. Through measures like the Muslim ban, the term 'citizen' acquires a cultural and religious connotation.[54] Likewise, the actual purpose of laws that curtail the rights of gays, lesbians and trans people and expose them to discrimination and threats of physical violence is not to protect *others from them*, nor have they anything to do with religious freedom or the protection of children and minors, as is typically alleged. The actual purpose of such laws is to dehumanize gays, lesbians and trans people and so to exclude them from the community of 'decent citizens'.

Now consider this issue in the broader context of identity management and security policy. What the Muslim ban does is to replace an individual vetting process for visa holders and visa applicants from the seven affected countries with a blanket prohibition. All citizens of these countries are labelled as potential terrorists. Structurally similar are many of the debates about the so-called bathroom bills, which deny many trans persons access to public toilets that correspond to their lived gender – allegedly to protect others from sexual harassment and assault.[55] What the public debate about these bills achieved was a replacement of individual instances of suspicion in public toilets with the notion that all trans persons – and this applied to both trans women and trans men, insofar as they used women's restrooms – could be 'men in drag' with nefarious intentions. In both cases, complex truths about immigrants, refugees, terrorists and terrorism, sexual assault, feelings of safety or insecurity public spaces were replaced with simplistic 'truthinesses':[56] asylum-seekers are potential terrorists; trans people are sexual predators in disguise.

It is not difficult to see why individual politicians and governments are tempted to govern by truthiness rather than reason and evidence. Like individual agents, states need to reduce complexity in order to be able to act. Bills and executive orders like the ones discussed earlier, which target groups rather than individuals, reduce complexity in the most drastic way. They presuppose simple explanations for social ills and offer simple solutions. And while reduction of complexity is *necessary* for a state to be able to function, and for the citizens to be able to trust it, the extreme reductionism that we see in the Muslim ban or in the 'bathroom bills' clearly represents a moral danger. This moral danger of reductionism can range from the relatively harmless to the genocidal.

The genocide of Europe's Jews would not have been possible without significant administrative efforts, and the Nazis were quite adept at combining violent propaganda with administrative zeal. Hitler's and Goebbels' propaganda sought to portray Jews as enemies of the German people, as responsible for the harsh conditions inflicted upon Germany after the First World War,[57] and as involved in an international cabal to bring down the sovereign nations of Europe. Legal discrimination and propaganda went hand in hand, both paving the way for the dehumanization and eventual destruction of the Jews. As we saw earlier, by 1940, propaganda films portrayed Jews as literal pests, while the deportations to Eastern Europe had begun and the Warsaw Ghetto was created.[58] In the Third Reich, a number of different laws and decrees provided the legal and administrative framework for the discrimination, segregation and eventual destruction of Jews, gradually removing any legal protection they had as citizens or residents. In 1935, the Nuremberg Race Laws (*Nürnberger Rassegesetze*) stripped German Jews of their citizenship and prohibited sexual relation between Jews and 'Germans' – this was called *Rassenschande*, literally: dishonouring one's race. In 1938, executive orders forced Jews to report property in excess of 5,000 Reichsmark for later confiscation[59] and to adopt the second name of Sara or Israel, if they had a 'non-Jewish' given name. In October 1938, the Ministry of the Interior invalidated all passports held by

German Jews and required that these passports be surrendered to the authorities and stamped with a red 'J' to revalidate them.[60] In 1939, Jews in occupied Poland were forced to wear the infamous yellow star (*Judenstern*); this requirement was extended to all German and German-occupied territories in 1941. The implementation of all these measures required significant administrative efforts and turned the bureaucracy of the German Reich against the Jewish population. The abominable end points of these efforts were the numbers tattooed onto prisoners' arms in the concentration camps and the inventories of the valuables taken from those who were murdered in Auschwitz-Birkenau or Treblinka. Without previous efforts to register Jews, to gradually exclude them from all public life, and to strip them of the liberties and legal protection afforded to other citizens, the logistical efforts of the Shoah would not have been possible. In order to destroy a population, one needs to know first who belongs to it and where one can find them. This point may seem trivial in comparison to the physical horrors of the Shoah, but it should not be disregarded. It was, after all, mid- and low-level bureaucrats who executed the anti-Semitic laws and decrees; and it was mid- and low-level bureaucrats who organized and maintained the infrastructure of the Shoah.

The Shoah is, of course, an extreme example, but it is nevertheless illuminating for our analysis of contemporary moral dangers. The Nazis operated with an efficient bureaucracy, stirring up nationalist hate against Jews, communists, socialists and against gays. They turned the administrative apparatus into a tool of their hate. The Nazi state was a mistrustful state with a hypochondriac identity; it defined itself by labelling certain groups as mortal enemies of the German nation. Germany's economic and social problems were blamed on the Jews and other minorities, and so curtailing, uprooting and eventually destroying these groups became palatable as official policy. Together with fairly generous social policies and ambitious military and civil engineering projects, this created the impression that the Nazi regime was actually taking steps towards improving conditions for 'ordinary' Germans. Explanations of German problems were simplified in much the same way that Luhmann suggests in his analysis of trust. The Nazi regime attempted to focus citizens' trust in the very person of Adolf Hitler and to direct their mistrust towards already marginalized groups. It explained the world in extremely simplistic terms in order to persuade ordinary people to mistrust any kind of cosmopolitanism or internationalism. The Nazis' 'reduction of complexity' ended in global war and genocide. Of course, not every political strategy to reduce complexity by sowing and exploiting mistrust need have lethal consequences.[61] Yet it is worth considering the moral and political risks such strategies can present. Defining legal and administrative measures in terms of group affiliation can provide a welcome shortcut for political agents. So for instance, instead of treating every traveller as a potential risk, which is time- and manpower-intensive, we can attempt to narrow down a circle of suspicious groups whose members receive extra attention. Such attention can take the form of bans, but they can also come in the seemingly more harmless shape of risk profiling. In either case, 'dangerous' qualities are defined primarily in terms of social, ethnic or religious belonging. Instead of considering information about the *individual* in question, information about the group they supposedly belong becomes decisive. In this way, epistemic trust is replaced with social trust or mistrust and actual or imagined group qualities serve as stand-ins for actual knowledge about an individual.

Now, as I suggested earlier, in the context of administrative tasks, police work and border control – where time and manpower are necessarily limited – knowledge about individuals can never be complete or perfect. Hence, hunches and social trust will always play a role, and as long as we have human administrators, there will always be a risk that their judgements will be biased. This should not be taken as a reason to dismiss all human judgement and strive for a completely automated administration – as we also saw, the expanding use of technology presents its own challenges. But it is a reason to pay close attention to *how* administrative systems are used by those with political and social power.

NOTES

1. I take the term 'archival knowledge' from Craig Robertson, 'A Documentary Regime of Verification: The Emergence of the US Passport and the Archival Problematization of Identity', *Cultural Studies* 23:3 (2009): 329–354.

2. I will discuss epistemic issues (especially issues of epistemic trust) in more detail further. Here, I simply want to note that I do *not* mean to imply that administrative knowledge is proper knowledge while intimate knowledge is not (or vice versa).

3. I would claim that everyone who has ever worked as a teacher knows how difficult this task is. In assessing pupils or students, teachers are supposed to be impartial – that is, they are not supposed to weigh particular considerations about their students unless these are relevant to the assessment of the task the students completed. Yet teachers receive personal appeals all the time, for extensions of deadlines, reconsiderations of grades and so forth – and it is very difficult, if not considered unprofessional to simply tell a student that details of their personal life are insignificant for their teacher.

4. Hannah Arendt, 'We Refugees', in *Altogether Elsewhere: Writers on Exile*, ed. Marc Robinson (Boston and London: Faber and Faber, 1994), 118–119.

5. Edmund L. Gettier, 'Is Justified True Belief Knowledge?' *Analysis* 23:6 (1963): 121–123. For an overview of the development of contemporary analytic epistemology and its current debates, see Matthias Steup, 'Epistemology', *The Stanford Encyclopedia of Philosophy* (Fall 2016 Edition), ed. Edward N. Zalta (Stanford: The

Metaphysics Research Lab, 2016), accessed 1 June 2017, https://plato.stanford.edu/entries/epistemology/.

6. To briefly illustrate why justification is so important: I could have a true belief about something – for instance, the belief that former Swedish Prime Minister Olof Palme was murdered by an American spy – without being able to justify this belief. As long as there is no hard evidence in the case – as long as the Palme murder remains unsolved – my belief remains a mere belief.

7. The discussion around the relative strengths and weaknesses of foundationalism and coherentism is broad and ongoing. I do not have the space here to go into any detail: all I want to show here is that when it comes to identity verification, administrative systems can exhibit both foundationalist and coherentist attitudes.

8. The second example alludes to Yahya Jammeh, the second president of the Gambia, who had ruled the country for twenty-two years when he lost the presidential election of 2016 to his challenger, Adama Barrow. Jammeh initially admitted defeat, then changed his mind, alleged voter fraud and refused to step down. He was eventually removed from office in a non-violent military intervention by other West African states in January 2017. When I first heard the news of Jammeh's defeat in the election, I could not believe it – and when he refused to hand over power to his elected successor, my initial reaction was 'Of course he wouldn't!' – because the turn of events seemed to confirm what I thought I knew about Jammeh and the political landscape of western Africa.

9. Today, photos and videos often play the part of 'basic facts' in such contexts, but we know – or in any case, should know – that these are vulnerable to manipulation and framing. That is, even 'direct' footage must often be considered in terms of their context, or in light of any editing process it might have undergone.

10. Erik Olsson, 'Coherentist Theories of Epistemic Justification', *Stanford Encyclopedia of Philosophy*, Spring 2014 Edition, ed. Edward N. Zalta (Stanford: The Metaphysics Research Lab, 2014), sect. 1, accessed 1 June 2017, https://plato.stanford.edu/entries/justep-coherence/.

11. For a thorough legal, moral and epistemic analysis of this issue, see Janna Weßels, 'Sexual Orientation in Refugee Status Determination', Refugee Studies Centre, Working Paper Series No. 74 (Oxford: University of Oxford, Department of International Development: 2011), accessed 6 February 2017, http://www.refworld.org/pdfid/55c9fe604.pdf.

12. Ghassam Kassisieh, *From Lives of Fear to Lives of Freedom: A Review of Australian Refugee Decisions on the Basis of Sexual Orientation* (Glebe, New South Wales: Gay and Lesbian Rights Lobby, 2008), 45–47.

13. This happened in the case of an Iranian lesbian, Samira Danesh, who was told by a lower administrative court that should could live in Iran without being bothered if she were discreet (Bayerisches Verwaltungsgericht Bayreuth, decision from 5 March 2012, file code B 3 K 11.30113); and in the case of a Nigerian man, where another administrative court suggested that he either 'live discreetly' or move to one of Nigeria's megacities in order to avoid the persecution he claimed to have endured in his rural home (Verwaltungsgericht Regensburg, decision from 7 October 2011, file code RN 5 K 11.30261).

14. Paisley Currah and Lisa Jean Moore, '"We Won't Know Who You Are": Contesting Sex Designation in New York City Birth Certificates', *Hypatia* 24:3 (2009): 113–135.

15. Currah and Moore, 'We Won't Know Who You Are', 118–126.

16. Lambda Legal, 'Changing Birth Certificate Sex Designations: State-by-State Guidelines', last updated on 3 February 2015, accessed on 17 March 2017, http://www.lambdalegal.org/know-your-rights/article/trans-changing-birth-certificate-sex-designations.

17. Emily Schmall, 'Transgender Advocates Hail Law Easing Rules in Argentina', *New York Times*, 24 May 2012, accessed 17 March 2017, http://www.nytimes.com/2012/05/25/world/americas/transgender-advocates-hail-argentina-law.html; Laws of Malta, *Gender Identity, Gender Expression, and Sex Characteristics Act*, 14 April 2015, accessed 17 March 2017, http://justiceservices.gov.mt/DownloadDocument.aspx?app=lom&itemid=12312&l=1; Emine Saner, 'Europe's Terrible Trans Rights Record: Will Denmark's New Law Spark Change?' *The Guardian*, 1 September 2014, accessed 17 March 2017, https://www.theguardian.com/society/shortcuts/2014/sep/01/europe-terrible-trans-rights-record-denmark-new-law.

18. Emilio Mordini and Sonia Massari, 'Body, Biometrics, and Identity', *Bioethics* 22:9 (2008): 495–497.

19. Mordini and Massari actually note the large number of children in developing countries whose birth goes unregistered and who, as a result, might never be able to acquire a legal identity; but they suggest that a global system of biometric identification could tackle the problem ('Body, Biometrics, and Identity', 497). While it is true that biometric identification is likely the only way forward for truly international systems of identification, I do not share their optimism about overcoming problems of access to such systems.

20. Jennifer Rankin, 'European Parliament Set to Pass Passenger Data Law', *The Guardian*, 13 April 2017, accessed 9 March 2017, https://www.theguardian.com/world/2016/apr/13/european-parliament-set-to-pass-passenger-data-law.

21. This is the ambition for the Automated Virtual Agent for Truth Assessments in Real Time (AVATAR), an automated border control and biometric lie detector. AVATAR was developed at the University of Arizona and has since moved to San Diego State University with its primary developer, Aaron Elkins. For a recent summary of the status of the project, see Suzanne Finch, 'The Lie-Detecting Security Kiosk of the Future', *SDSU NewsCenter*, 16 December 2016, accessed 6 February 2017, http://newscenter.sdsu.edu/sdsu_newscenter/news_story.aspx?sid=76505.

22. Emerging research on the role of biases in academia can be brought to bear on this issue, see, for instance, Gabriella Gutiérrez y Muhs et al., eds., *Presumed Incompetent: The Intersections of Race and Class for Women in Academia* (Logan: Utah State University Press, 2012).

23. This issue is explored under the heading of *epistemic injustice* by Miranda Fricker (*Epistemic Injustice: Power and the Ethics of Knowing*, Oxford: Oxford University Press 2007) and generally within the field of *social epistemology* (for an overview, see Alvin Goldman and Thomas Blanchard, 'Social Epistemology', *Stanford Encyclopedia of Philosophy*, Winter 2016 edition, ed. Edward N. Zalta (Stanford: The

Metaphysics Research Lab 2016), accessed 1 June 2017, https://plato.stanford.edu/entries/epistemology-social/.

24. At a social event after a biometry conference, a security specialist once told me that there was no way engineers could anticipate all the ways in which people struggle with even the most straightforward designs.

25. See for instance, this publicly accessible presentation by Dmitry O. Gorodnichy et al.: 'Automated Border Control Systems as Part of e-Border Crossing Process', NIST International Biometric Performance Conference (IBPC 2014), accessed 1 June 2017, https://www.nist.gov/sites/default/files/documents/2016/12/01/14-nist-abc-eborder-gorodnichy.p.pdf.

26. Note that I am not advancing the claim that any such system is necessarily biased. I am merely advancing the weaker claim that there is a non-trivial risk of perpetuating such biases.

27. Carolin Emcke, *Gegen den Hass* (Frankfurt am Main: S. Fischer, 2016). All translations are mine.

28. Most of her analysis focuses on Germany. She also discusses the propaganda of the so-called Islamic State and the case of the United States – one chapter of the book is devoted to the case of Eric Garner's death at the hands of police and systemic racism – but I take it that the part of her argument that I will focus on here can be applied to other countries that have been experiencing a nationalist backlash over the past years.

29. Emcke, *Gegen den Hass*, 188.

30. There is a tradition of 'liberal nationalism' in Anglophone political philosophy; see, for instance, David Miller, *On Nationality* (Oxford: Clarendon Press, 1995) or Yael Tamir, *Liberal Nationalism* (Princeton: Princeton University Press, 1995). Here I remain agnostic on the question whether liberal nationalism is possible at all or whether nationalism must always have illiberal elements. The nationalism whose return we are now witnessing into mainstream politics in both North America and Europe clearly has illiberal aims: it is not interested in the protection of equal rights, inclusion and international cooperation.

31. Emcke, *Gegen den Hass*, 121: 'The figure of speech that treats a society like a body triggers associations that have political consequences: a body is enclosed and limited by skin. A body is vulnerable to illnesses causes by germs and bacteria. A body needs to be healthy and protected from epidemics. But most of all, a body is a homogeneous whole.'

32. MDR Sachsen-Anhalt, 'Entsetzen im Landtag über Poggenburg" ('State Parliament shocked by Poggenburg's remarks'), last updated on 4 February 2017, accessed on 19 March 2017, http://www.mdr.de/sachsen-anhalt/landespolitik/poggenburg-eklat-landtag-100.html.

33. Emcke, *Gegen den Hass*, 121.

34. Emcke, *Gegen den Hass*, 122.

35. I do not mean to imply that there are no ways to rationally and civilly criticize anti-racists, feminists or queer activists – which should be obvious from the fact that these groups are not homogenous and often disagree about political strategy among and within each other. The point here is to emphasize just how over the top the hypochondriac's attitude is.

36. Ongoing, that is, in several federal states, as education policy in Germany is not a federal matter but a state matter.

37. An overview of the immediate reactions to and confusion stemming from the order can be found in *The Guardian*: Alan Yuhas and Mazin Sidhamed, 'Is This a Muslim Ban? Trump's Executive Order Explained', last updated 31 January 2017, accessed 7 February 2017, https://www.theguardian.com/us-news/2017/jan/28/trump-immigration-ban-syria-muslims-reaction-lawsuits.

38. Uri Friedman, 'Where American Terrorists Actually Come From', *The Atlantic*, last updated 30 January 2017, accessed 7 February 2017, https://www.theatlantic.com/international/archive/2017/01/trump-immigration-ban-terrorism/514361/. Friedman's article relies heavily on the research of Alex Nowrasteh, an immigration researcher at the libertarian Cato Institute.

39. Cf. note 67 in chapter 2.

40. Some of these attacks are detailed and analysed in a commentary by the scientific advisory board of the *Institut für Sexualpädagogik Dortmund* (Institute for Sexual Pedagogy, isp): Philipps, Ina-Maria et al., 'Kampagnen gegen emanzipatorische sexuelle Bildung' ('Campaigns against progressive sexual education'), *Zeitschrift für Sexualforschung* 29 (2016): 73–89.

41. What I say here about Trump and the German debate about sexual education can also be applied to political discourse regarding refugees in Germany and other European countries. I chose sexual education as my European example, since I want to emphasize the common source of these apocalyptic visions, whether they concern immigrants or queers.

42. Voices on the extreme right have described Germany's acceptance of hundreds of thousands of Syrian refugees in 2015 as *Umvolkung*, another Nazi term (literally: ethnic replacement, in the current political context suggesting a plan to replace the ethnic German population with refugees).

43. Luhmann, Niklas: *Vertrauen*, 5th edition (München and Konstanz: UVK Verlagsgesellschaft, 2014), 27–38. All translations are mine; there is an English translation of the work (Part I in *Trust and Power*, trans. Howard Davies, John Raffan and Kathryn Rooney, ed. Michael King and Christian Morgner) forthcoming by Wiley-Polity, but since the currently available English version is rather dated, I chose to work with the updated edition of the German original.

44. Luhmann (*Vertrauen*, 1) kicks off the book with this dramatic statement: 'Trust . . . is an essential element of social life. Human beings often have a choice on whether to trust someone or something. But without any trust, you could not leave your bed in the morning. A vague fear and paralyzing dread would befall you. You could not even ground your defensive efforts in specific forms of mistrust, since that would require that you trust in other respects. Everything would be possible. No human being could withstand being confronted with the world's utter complexity for long'. On the same theme, cf. Marek Kohn, *Trust: Self-Interest and the Common Good* (Oxford: Oxford University Press 2008), ch. 1.

45. Derek Lowe, a chemist who engages in both professional and political commentary on his widely read blog *In the Pipeline*, has written an insightful analysis of 'pro-natural' and 'anti-chemical' rhetoric and of how chemists can engage with it productively: 'All Natural and Chemical Free', 2 July 2014, accessed 20 March 2017, http://blogs.sciencemag.org/pipeline/archives/2014/07/02/all_natural_and_chemical_free.

46. This assumption is, of course, defeasible: Doctors or carpenters may turn out to be incompetent, and search engines may skew results. The point here is not to claim that these assumptions are always going to be epistemically warranted but to show how they generally make our lives easier.

47. Luhmann, *Vertrauen*, 95.

48. In the early fall of 2014, several news outlets picked up a story about alleged fraud and infighting at a libertarian commune founded by American investors near Santiago, Galt's Gulch Chile. For a long-form account, see Harry Cheadle, 'Atlas Mugged: How a Libertarian Paradise in Chile Fell Apart', *Vice*, 22 September 2014, accessed 7 February 2017: https://www.vice.com/en_us/article/atlas-mugged-922-v21n10.

49. Luhmann, *Vertrauen*, 92.

50. The acronym PEGIDA stands for 'Patriotic Europeans for the Defense of the Occident'. The PEGIDA marches began in late 2014 in Dresden and quickly spread to other cities. They hit their peak in 2015 and early 2016, but their turnout has been dwindling since.

51. This sentiment became prominent even among wider segments of the population after the sexual attacks in Cologne on New Year's Eve 2015/16. The police did not release any statement relating to the attacks until 2 January, and national media only began to report the mass assaults that had occurred on the Cathedral Square on 4 January 2016, at which point the police came under fire for their information policy. Many social media users assumed that the delay in reporting the events was due to a deliberate political cover-up, since the majority of the alleged perpetrators were assumed to be asylum-seekers from North African countries. While the police arguably mishandled the situation on the square, the view that there was a cover-up is debunked in Jan Bielicki, 'Warum die Medien so spät über Köln berichteten' ('Why it took the media so long to report on Cologne'), *Süddeutsche Zeitung*, 7 January 2016, accessed 24 March 2017: http://www.sueddeutsche.de/medien/uebergriffe-an-silvester-warum-die-medien-so-spaet-ueber-koeln-berichteten-1.2808386.

52. Luhmann describes both trust and mistrust as social feedback loops (*Vertrauen*, 98–99).

53. Luhmann, *Vertrauen*, 93.

54. To be clear, this is not a new development in U.S. immigration policy. The tendency to regulate immigration to the United States according to whichever group tends to be perceived as a scapegoat for American problems or as a threat to American interests goes back to at least the Chinese Exclusion Act of 1882, continued with the racist quota policies in effect from the 1920s to the 1960s, and had one of its darkest moments when the United States turned away Jewish refugees from Europe just before the Second World War broke out.

55. Schilt and Westbrook, 'Bathroom Battleground and Penis Panics'.

56. American comedian Stephen Colbert coined the term – in its current meaning of 'perceived truth, bullshit' – on his satirical news show *The Colbert Report*. To me, it seems most fitting to describe what I have in mind here: uttering something that merely 'feels true' without caring in the least about its actual truth value.

57. This myth – known by the German term *Dolchstoßlegende*, the legend of the 'stab in the back' – was popular not just among Nazis but also among conservative and military circles in the Weimar Republic. The *Dolchstoßlegende* claimed that

Germany lost the First World War because of internal strife and unrest caused by minorities and socialists.

58. Bundeszentrale für politische Bildung, 'Film im NS-Staat' ('Cinema in the Nazi State'), last updated 5 August 2013, accessed 21 March 2017, http://www.bpb.de/geschichte/nationalsozialismus/geheimsache-ghettofilm/153344/film-im-ns-staat.

59. In 1939, another executive order forced Jews to surrender all valuables – precious metals and precious stones – to the state without compensation.

60. A timeline of anti-Semitic legislation in Nazi Germany, from which the information summarized here is gleaned, can be found on the homepage of the United States Holocaust Memorial Museum, accessed 2 February 2017, https://www.ushmm.org/wlc/en/article.php?ModuleId=10007901.

61. Although there are numerous examples where it does: from recent history, the civil wars in Yugoslavia and Rwanda in the 1990s and Pol Pot's regime in Cambodia fall into this category.

Chapter 5

Conclusion

The task that remains is threefold: First, to recap the argument that I have developed in the course of this book; second, to detail some of the moral and political challenges that stem from the account proposed here; and third, to indicate some avenues for further research. In the most general terms, what I have proposed here is a relational account of personal identity. Rather than locating the source of identity in 'intrinsic' criteria such as bodily or mental continuity, I have argued that it is constituted by social processes. Many of the thinkers we have encountered treated personal identity as if it were a purely descriptive concept and go on to argue that, since it does not properly describe any real thing, personal identity is a fiction. In contrast, I suggested that this concept is normative rather than descriptive: that it tracks specific ways of relating to the world and to each other. It is the notion of personal identity that makes it possible to hold one another responsible for our actions or to claim our rights vis-à-vis other people or one's government. It is through this concept that we constitute ourselves as moral, legal and political subjects. This normative character also makes the concept of personal identity – and by extension the concept of social identity – a moral, legal and political battleground. While the state can be subject to criticism for the ways in which it applies its identity management schemes to individuals, the social realities of our world – such as accelerating urbanization, centralized administration and transnational integration and migration – make official identification at once a political necessity and a moral good.

While mutual recognition among intimates and in close-knit communities is important and a topic wholly deserving of the philosophical attention it has received, it does not and cannot play the role of official or state identification. But although such identification is essential, it has received comparatively little philosophical attention. So before anything else, this book is a plea to treat matters of official identification – and official recognition – as worthy of serious philosophical reflection. Before I sketch the direction in which I think this reflection ought to proceed, let me briefly summarize the basis on which I do so.

In the first chapter, I claimed that philosophical analysis of personal identity must consider the social environment in which identity claims are launched and either accepted or rejected. Crucially, this social environment includes more than just the intimate contexts of families, friendships and close-knit communities; it extends to the state's activities in identity management. Against philosophers who argue that personal identity is an illusion, or that it does not matter, I argued for the primacy of the practical: metaphysical efforts to understand the nature of personal identity must not ignore the moral, political and legal significance of the concept – either by trying to dismiss it as a mere construction, or by trying to separate it from supposedly 'pure' metaphysical questions about the endurance of human animals and human minds. For since our selfhood is embedded in our social world, so is our identity.

In chapter two, we saw how the narrative theorists of personal identity expanded the analytical approach of modern and contemporary metaphysics to include social and ethical questions. I suggested, however, that a broader understanding of 'narrative' is needed than is commonly espoused by the narrativists; namely one that includes an understanding of the administrative and legal processes by which identities are created, affirmed or denied. That required that the bulk of the chapter be devoted to replying to objections to the narrativist view: that it does not conform to the lived experience of 'non-narrativist' types and that it undercuts the epistemic criteria we should want to apply to identity claims – in other words, that it makes such claims susceptible to embellishment and invention. I suggested that the way out here is to embrace the normative character of the narrativist account, not to dismiss it. Narratives – personal as well as official ones – are constructed in social environments with power differentials and the construction of these narratives tracks social (and sometimes legal) norms. Recognizing this, in turn, opens up these power differentials and these norms for moral questioning. Embellishment and invention remain a clear danger, but it is one that may be circumvented by paying attention to the realities of power. That task is what underlies the story that follows.

In chapter three, I took a closer look at the reasons why states engage in identity management in the first place and how they assume this power over their subjects. Following James C. Scott's notion of 'seeing like a state', I described identity management as the expression of a modern logic that aims for comprehensive yet shallow knowledge of its objects – in order to govern efficiently. The modern state needs to be able to know its subjects in an impersonal, standardized way: as tax-payers, soldiers, welfare recipients and so on. This way of knowing is not necessarily alienating or harmful. But it clearly carries moral and political risks. Official identities can provide a person with the authority to claim his or her rights and demand respect, but they can also be used to deny rights and to expose people to oppression and violence. These risks are especially pronounced where people are being administered not as individuals but as members of a group; or not being recognized at all, because they do not belong either to a recognizable group or to one deemed recognizable.

In the fourth chapter, I further spelled out this concern. States and their agents need to trust people who they do not know intimately. Such trust is established through identity management and record-keeping. But two factors complicate the matter: first, trust has different dimensions that can come into conflict with each other (e.g., social trust can undermine epistemic trust). Second, while identity management may aspire to the status of a closed system of perfect knowledge, it has to work under imperfect conditions (e.g., where people lose their documents). This allows for dangerous perversions of identity management that seek not to establish trust but to exploit and embellish mistrust. Where such mistrust is weaponized by political interests and the administration, this can have serious, even lethal, consequences.

The identity management efforts of states are a direct exercise of power: citizens and residents are categorized, and their categorization determines what rights they can claim and what services they may have access to. While this exercise of power must be critically observed, it need not on that account be condemned just because it expresses a power differential. Narratives in intimate contexts can be insulting and harmful; or they can be empowering. But while we can and should, as individuals, resist insulting and harmful narratives – both in terms of being subjected to them and in terms of applying them – we do not get to define ourselves *ex nihilo*. The same applies to the relationship of the individual with their country of residence or citizenship: the state has the potential both to empower the individual and to diminish and marginalize them. But to presume that the state's efforts to create and maintain official identities must per se be an exercise in domination is simply to rule out a more nuanced perspective on the administrative realities we navigate. And that is a mistake. If we suppose that all identity management systems are informed by a political will to surveil and control, then we deprive ourselves of the opportunity to distinguish actors who use their power responsibly from those who do not. Take the role of the birth certificate in modern identity management: as a 'breeder document', it is the cornerstone of official recognition. The fact that, globally, a third of all children under five years[1] were not registered at birth is an enormous injustice, considering the importance of early registration in modern administrative infrastructure.

This injustice cannot be addressed by a sweeping rejection of all identity management, nor by sweeping global solutions we might be unable to implement – politically or logistically – for tens or hundreds of years. It needs a solution that works under imperfect conditions and is open to gradual amendment and improvement as the situation changes.

Identity management is the focal point of a number of morally significant interests: an interest in security against fraud and terrorist attack, in efficient and dignified interactions with the agents and institutions of the state, in the protection of private information from these same agents and institutions and in not being *mis*represented. Compromises between these different interests are not always going to be easy to reach; and the notion of misrepresentation in particular might look like an obvious source of philosophical trouble: for if I am correct to claim that identity consists in 'being recognized as', then by what criteria are we to distinguish recognition from misrepresentation? To put the question in more concrete terms: if I consider myself as non-binary, but everyone else regards me as either a man or a woman – *and* if I really am what I am being recognized as and not what *I think* I am – then how could I claim that I am being misrepresented? Note that unlike, say, a blatant lie on my CV, this is not the kind of identity claim that can be proven or disproven by an appeal to a set of independently verifiable facts. In the absence of such facts, the answer to the question of whether I am being misrepresented – or indeed whether I am misrepresenting myself – hinges on two things. First, whether 'non-binary' is a socially available identity category, that is, an identity category that other people can in principle understand and use; and second, whether there is an overriding interest that would preclude others from using this category and justify their continued exclusive use of the identity categories 'man' and 'woman'. Without delving further into a discussion of sexual identity categories, I propose that 'non-binary' is a socially available identity category[2] and that there is no overriding interest in classifying people as either men or women – which makes this case different from one where I state my nationality as 'Klingon' properly to reflect my fondness for science fiction and the martial arts.

Of course, whether an identity category is socially available is itself dependent on larger socio-political developments; and often the conflicts that emerge here are precisely about whether particular categories *should* be socially available or not (conflicts about 'third gender' or 'agender' categories' are one example). Yet these conflicts are themselves open to moral scrutiny in the sense that we can ask, 'Whose interests are at stake here? Which of these have more weight? Can a compromise between them be reached or does one need to be prioritized over the other? What are the costs of such prioritization?' I shall not develop a precise metric for weighing these interests here, but I hope that the various examples I have discussed give an indication where such a metric could take its starting point: by looking at cases where interests are cruelly and malevolently disregarded, and where misrecognition paves the way for marginalization and violence.

This book, then, has sought to bridge the gap between 'strictly metaphysical' and 'strictly practical' thinking about identity. However, the model of personal identity I develop here is not to be taken as the 'final word' on the matter. Rather, I hope to encourage social scientists, metaphysicians, moral and political philosophers and others to look more closely at administrative practices. Within the space of this book, I can only sketch some of the processes that seem to me relevant to a more fruitful understanding of identity and to a productive critique of state agency. Future work in this field might pick up these 'sketches' and use them for more detailed normative analyses than I provide here – comparatively, historically or in light of social and technological developments that are yet to come. It would be impudent to predict these developments, but I hope nonetheless that the argument presented here can provide a framework for making sense of them in light of that which is right now and that which came before.

NOTES

1. Lene Mikkelsen et al., 'A Global Assessment of Civil Registration and Vital Statistics Systems: Monitoring Data Quality and Progress', *The Lancet* 386 (2015): 1395–1406.

2. In a more detailed discussion of this specific issue, this claim would, of course, need to be qualified regarding the particular geographical, historical and social location in question: 'non-binary' may be intelligible in, for example, the United Kingdom and Germany but perhaps not in other countries.

Bibliography

BOOKS AND ARTICLES

Aas, Katja Franko. ' "The Body Does Not Lie": Identity, Risk, and Trust in Technoculture'. *Crime, Media, Culture* 2 (2006): 143–158.
Aas, Katja Franko and Mary Bosworth, editors. *The Borders of Punishment: Migration, Citizenship, and Social Exclusion*. Oxford: Oxford University Press, 2013.
Ajana, Btihaj. 'Biometric Citizenship'. *Citizenship Studies* 16:7 (2012): 851–870.
Ajana, Btihaj 'Recombinant Identities'. *Bioethical Inquiry* 7 (2010): 237–258.
Alterman, Anton. ' "A Piece of Yourself": Ethical Issues in Biometric Identification'. *Ethics and Information Technology* 5:3 (2003): 139–150
Amoore, Louise. 'Biometric Borders: Governing Mobilities in the War on Terror'. *Political Geography* 25 (2006): 336–351.
Anderson, Benedict. *Imagined Communities: Reflections on the Origin and Spread of Nationalism*, revised edition. London and New York: Verso Books, 2006.
Arendt, Hannah. 'We Refugees'. In *Altogether Elsewhere: Writers on Exile*, edited by Marc Robinson, 110–119. Boston and London: Faber and Faber, 1994.
Ásta Kristjana Sveinsdóttir. 'The Metaphysics of Sex and Gender'. In *Feminist Metaphysics*, edited by Charlotte Witt, 47–65. Dordrecht: Springer, 2011.
Baker, Lynne Rudder. 'Making Sense of Ourselves: Self-Narratives and Personal Identity'. *Phenomenology and the Cognitive Sciences* 15 (2016): 7–15.
Barker, Stephanie, Stefankai Spoerlein, Tobias Vetter and Wolfgang Viereck. *An Atlas of English Surnames*. Frankfurt am Main: Peter Lang, 2007.
Behrensen, Maren. 'Identity as Convention: Biometric Passports and the Promise of Security'. *Journal of Information, Communication and Ethics in Society* 12:1 (2014): 44–59.
Behrensen, Maren. 'In the Halfway House of Ill-Repute: Gender Verification under a Different Name, Still no Contribution to Fair Play'. *Sport, Ethics, and Philosophy* 7:4 (2013): 450–466.

Bettcher, Talia Mae. 'Evil Deceivers and Make-Believers: On Transphobic Violence and the Politics of Illusion'. *Hypatia* 22 (2007): 43–65.

Brecher, Bob. *Torture and the Ticking Bomb*. Malden: Blackwell, 2007.

Buitelaar, J. C. 'Privacy and Narrativity in the Internet Era'. *The Information Society* 30:4 (2014): 266–281.

Cahn, Susan. 'Testing Sex, Attributing Gender: What Caster Semenya Means to Women's Sports'. *Journal of Intercollegiate Sport* 4 (2011): 38–48.

Cheadle, Harry. 'Atlas Mugged: How a Libertarian Paradise in Chile Fell Apart'. *Vice*, 22 September 2014. Accessed 7 February 2017. https://www.vice.com/en_us/article/atlas-mugged-922-v21n10.

Ciralsky, Adam. 'The Celebrity Surgeon who Used Love, Money and the Pope to Scam an NBC News Producer'. *Vanity Fair*, 5 January 2016. Accessed 2 October 2016. http://www.vanityfair.com/news/2016/01/celebrity-surgeon-nbc-news-producer-scam.

Cochran, Moncrieff M. and Jane Anthony Brassard. 'Child Development and Personal Social Networks'. *Child Development* 50:3 (1979): 601–616.

Cole, Simon A. *Suspect Identities: A History of Fingerprinting and Criminal Identification*. Cambridge and London: Harvard University Press, 2001.

Currah, Paisley and Lisa Jean Moore. '"We Won't Know Who You Are": Contesting Sex Designation in New York City Birth Certificates'. *Hypatia* 24:3 (2009): 113–135.

Currah, Paisley and Tara Mulqueen. 'Securitizing Gender. Identity, Biometrics, and Transgender Bodies at the Airport'. *Social Research* 78:2 (2011): 557–582.

DeGrazia, David. 'Enhancement, and Self-Creation'. *The Hastings Center Report* 30:2 (2000): 34–40.

Eklund, Niklas. 'Administrative Reform in Sweden: Administrative Dualism at the Crossroad'. In *Handbook of Administrative Reform: An International Perspective*, edited by Jerri Killian and Niklas Eklund, 115–136. Boca Raton: CRC Press, 2008.

Emcke, Carolin. *Gegen den Hass*. Frankfurt am Main: S. Fischer, 2016.

Erikson, Erik H. *Childhood and Society*, second, revised edition. Harmondsworth: Penguin Books, 1965.

Erikson, Erik H. 'Identity and the Life Cycle: Selected Papers'. In *Psychological Issues*, vol. 1, edited by George S. Klein, vol. 1. New York: International Universities Press, 1959.

Ferrara, Matteo, Annalisa Franco and Davide Maltoni. 'The Magic Passport'. *IEEE International Joint Conference on Biometrics*, 29 September–2 October 2014, available on *IEEE Xplore*, DOI: 10.1109/BTAS.2014.6996240.

Fokker, A. A. 'Expressive Derivation of Proper Names in Russian'. *Lingua* 9 (1961): 267–276.

Foucault, Michel. *Discipline and Punish: The Birth of the Prison*, translated by Alan Sheridan, second edition. New York: Vintage Books, 1995.

Freedman, Terry and Iseabail Macleod. *The Wordsworth Dictionary of Surnames*. Ware: Wordsworth Reference, 1997.

Fricker, Miranda. *Epistemic Injustice: Power and the Ethics of Knowing*. Oxford: Oxford University Press, 2007.

Gettier, Edmund L. 'Is Justified True Belief Knowledge?' *Analysis* 23:6 (1963): 121–123.

Goffman, Erving. *The Presentation of Self in Everyday Life*. London: Penguin Books, 1990.
Gold, Ian and Lauren Olin. 'From Descartes to Desipramine: Psychopharmacology and the Self'. *Transcultural Psychology* 46:1 (2009): 38–59.
Goldman, Alvin and Thomas Blanchard. 'Social Epistemology'. *Stanford Encyclopedia of Philosophy*, Winter 2016 edition, edited by Edward N. Zalta. Stanford: The Metaphysics Research Lab, 2016.
Gottschald, Max. *Deutsche Namenskunde: Unsere Familiennamen*, 5th improved edition with an introduction by Rudolf Schützeichel. Berlin and New York: Walter de Gruyter, 1982.
Gutiérrez y Muhs, Gabriella, Yolanda Flores Niemann, Carmen G. Gonzalez and Angela P. Harris, editors. *Presumed Incompetent: The Intersections of Race and Class for Women in Academia*. Logan: Utah State University Press, 2012.
Heckscher, Sten, Ingrid Carlberg and Carl Gahmberg. *Karolinska Institutet and the Macchiarini Case: A Summary in English and Swedish*. Stockholm: E-Tryck AB, 2016. Accessed 2 October 2016. http://ki.se/sites/default/files/karolinska_institutet_and_the_macchiarini_case_summary_in_english_and_swedish.pdf.
Heimo, Olli I., Antti Hakkala and Kai K. Kimppa. 'How to Abuse Biometric Passport Systems'. *Journal of Information, Communication and Ethics in Society* 10:2 (2012): 68–81.
Hume, David. *Treatise of Human Nature*, edited by David F. Norton and Mary J. Norton. Oxford: Oxford University Press, 2000.
Kaganoff, Benzion C. 'Jewish Surnames through the Ages: An Etymological History'. *Commentary* 22:3 (1956): 249–259.
Kahn, Jeffrey. *Mrs. Shipley's Ghost: The Right to Travel and Terrorist Watchlists*. Ann Arbor: The University of Michigan Press, 2013.
Kant, Immanuel. *Critique of Pure Reason*, translated by Norman Kemp Smith. Basingstoke and London: Macmillan, 1990.
Karkazis, Katrina, Rebecca Jordan-Young, Georgiann Davis and Silvia Camporesi. 'Out of Bounds? A Critique of the New Policies on Hyperandrogenism in Elite Female Athletes'. *The American Journal of Bioethics* 12:7 (2012): 3–16.
Kassisieh, Ghassam. *From Lives of Fear to Lives of Freedom: A Review of Australian Refugee Decisions on the Basis of Sexual Orientation*. Glebe, New South Wales: Gay and Lesbian Rights Lobby, 2008.
Kohn, Marek. *Trust: Self-Interest and the Common Good*. Oxford: Oxford University Press, 2008.
Korsgaard, Christine. *Self-Constitution: Agency, Identity, and Integrity*. Oxford: Oxford University Press, 2009.
Lamb, David. 'Autonomy and the Refusal of Life-Prolonging Therapy'. *Res Publica* 1:2 (1995): 147–162.
Langton, Rae. 'Duty and Desolation'. *Philosophy* 67 (1992): 481–505.
Lewis, David. 'Survival and Identity'. In *Philosophical Papers*, vol. 1, 55–77. Oxford: Oxford University Press, 1983.
Lindemann, Hilde. *Holding and Letting Go: The Social Practice of Personal Identities*. Oxford: Oxford University Press, 2014.

Lippert, Randy. 'Governing Refugees: The Relevance of Governmentality to Understanding the International Refugee Regime'. *Alternatives* 24 (1999): 295–328.

Locke, John. *An Essay Concerning Human Understanding*, edited by Peter H. Nidditch. Oxford: Clarendon Press 1975.

Ludvigsson, Jonas F., Petra Otterblad-Olausson, Birgitta U. Pettersson and Anders Ekbom. 'The Swedish Personal Identity Number: Possibilities and Pitfalls in Healthcare and Medical Research'. *European Journal of Epidemiology* 24 (2009): 659–667.

Luhmann, Niklas. *Trust and Power*, translated by Howard Davies, John Raffan and Kathryn Rooney, edited by Michael King and Christian Morgner. Cambridge, Oxford, Boston and New York: Wiley-Polity, forthcoming.

Luhmann, Niklas. *Vertrauen*, 5th edition. München and Konstanz: UVK Verlagsgesellschaft, 2014.

Lyon, David. 'Biometrics, Identification, and Surveillance'. *Bioethics* 22:9 (2008): 499–508.

Lyon, David, editor. *Surveillance as Social Sorting: Privacy, Risk, and Digital Discrimination*. London and New York: Routledge, 2003.

Lyon, David. 'Surveillance, Security, and Social Sorting'. *International Criminal Justice Review* 17:3 (2007): 161–170.

MacIntyre, Alasdair. *After Virtue*, second edition. London: Duckworth, 1985.

Martin, Luther H., Huck Gutman and Patrick H. Hutton, editors. *Technologies of the Self: A Seminar with Michel Foucault*. London: Tavistock Publications, 1988.

McAdams, Dan P. and Kate C. McLean. 'Narrative Identity'. *Current Directions in Psychological Science* 22:3 (2013): 233–238.

Mikkelsen, Lene, David E. Phillips, Carla AbouZahr, David W. Setel, Don de Savigny, Rafael Lozano and Alan D. Lopez. 'A Global Assessment of Civil Registration and Vital Statistics Systems: Monitoring Data Quality and Progress'. *The Lancet* 386 (2015): 1395–1406.

Mikkola, Mari. 'Ontological Commitments, Sex, and Gender'. In *Feminist Metaphysics*, edited by Charlotte Witt, 67–83. Dordrecht: Springer, 2011.

Miller, David. *On Nationality*. Oxford: Clarendon Press, 1995.

Mordini, Emilio and Sonia Massari. 'Body, Biometrics, and Identity'. *Bioethics* 22:9 (2008): 488–498.

Mühlhäusler, Peter and Rom Harré. *Pronouns and People: The Linguistic Construction of Social and Personal Identity*. Oxford: Basil Blackwell, 1990.

Müller, Sabine, Merlin Bittlinger and Henrik Walter. 'Threats to Neurosurgical Patients Posed by the Personal Identity Debate'. *Neuroethics*, online first (21 January 2017), DOI: 10.1007/s12152-017-9304-0.

Munsell, Joel, editor. *Cases of Personal Identity*. Albany: Self-published, 1854.

Olson, Eric. *What Are We?* Oxford: Oxford University Press, 2007.

Olsson, Erik. 'Coherentist Theories of Epistemic Justification'. In *Stanford Encyclopedia of Philosophy* (Spring 2014 Edition), edited by Edward N. Zalta. Stanford: The Metaphysics Research Lab, 2014.

Parfit, Derek. *Reasons and Persons*. Oxford: Clarendon Press, 1984.

Philipps, Ina-Maria, Ulrike Schmauch, Uwe Sielert, Karlheinz Valtl and Joachim Walter. 'Kampagnen gegen emanzipatorische sexuelle Bildung: Stellungnahme

des Wissenschaftlichen Beirats des Instituts für Sexualpädagogik Dortmund (isp)'. *Zeitschrift für Sexualforschung* 29 (2016): 73–89.
Plakans, Andrejs and Charles Wetherell. 'Patrilines, Surnames and Family Identity'. *The History of the Family* 5:2 (2000): 199–214.
Quante, Michael. *Person*. Berlin and New York: Walter de Gruyter, 2007.
Quante, Michael. 'The Social Nature of Personal Identity'. *Journal of Consciousness Studies* 14:5–6 (2007): 56–76.
Rahe, Thomas. 'Polnische und jüdische Displaced Persons im DP-Camp Bergen-Belsen'. In *Jahresbericht 2015: Schwerpunktthema Flucht, Migration, Exil*, edited by Stiftung Niedersächsische Gedenkstätten, 10–17. Accessed 1 April 2017, http://www.stiftung-ng.de/fileadmin/dateien/Stiftung/Grafik_SNG/6.0.Publikationen/SNG_Jahresbericht_2015-web.pdf.
Reid, Thomas. *Essays on the Intellectual Powers of Man*, edited by Derek R. Brookes. University Park: Pennsylvania State University Press, 2002.
Robertson, Craig. 'A Documentary Regime of Verification: The Emergence of the US Passport and the Archival Problematization of Identity'. *Cultural Studies* 23:3 (2009): 329–354.
Rose, Nikolas. *Governing the Soul: The Shaping of the Private Self*, second edition. London and New York: Free Association Books, 1999.
Rudder Baker, Lynne 'Making Sense of Ourselves: Self-Narratives and Personal Identity'. *Phenomenology and the Cognitive Sciences* 15 (2016): 7–15.
Saramago, José. *All the Names*, translated by Margaret Jull Costa. London: The Harvill Press, 1999.
Schechtman, Marya. *The Constitution of Selves*. Ithaca: Cornell University Press, 1996.
Schechtman, Marya. *Staying Alive: Personal Identity, Practical Concerns, and the Unity of a Life*. Oxford: Oxford University Press, 2014.
Schilt, Kristen and Laurel Westbrook. 'Bathroom Battleground and Penis Panics'. *Contexts* 14:3 (2015): 26–31.
Scott, James C. *Seeing Like a State: How Certain Schemes to Improve the Human Condition Have Failed*. New Haven and London: Yale University Press, 2008.
Shoemaker, Sydney. 'Personal Identity: A Materialist Account'. In *Metaphysics: The Big Questions*, edited by Peter van Inwagen and Dean W. Zimmerman, 296–310. Malden, Mass.: Blackwell Publishing, 1998.
Sigvardsdotter, Erika. *Presenting the Absent: An Account of Undocumentedness in Sweden*. Dissertation, Uppsala: Kulturgeografiska institutionen, Uppsala universitet, 2012.
Stankiewicz, Edward. 'The Expression of Affection in Russian Proper Names'. *The Slavic and East European Journal* 1:3 (1957): 196–210.
Statistiska Centralbyrån. *Bakgrundsfakta Befolknings- och välfärdsstatistik 2016:1, Personnummer*, Örebro: Statistiska Centralbyrån, 2016.
Steup, Matthias. 'Epistemology'. In *The Stanford Encyclopedia of Philosophy* (Fall 2016 Edition), edited by Edward N. Zalta. Stanford: The Metaphysics Research Lab, 2016.
Strawson, Galen. 'Against Narrativity'. *Ratio* 17 (2004): 428–452.

Strawson, Galen. 'I Am Not a Story'. *Aeon*, 3 September 2015. Accessed 2 October 2016: https://aeon.co/essays/let-s-ditch-the-dangerous-idea-that-life-is-a-story.
Strawson, Peter. *Individuals: An Essay in Descriptive Metaphysics*, digital reprint. London and New York: Routledge, 2011.
Swinburne, Richard. 'Personal Identity: The Dualist Theory'. In *Metaphysics: The Big Questions*, edited by Peter van Inwagen and Dean W. Zimmerman, 317–333. Malden: Blackwell Publishing, 1998.
Tamir, Yael. *Liberal Nationalism*. Princeton: Princeton University Press, 1995.
Taylor, Charles. 'The Politics of Recognition'. In *Multiculturalism*, edited by Amy Gutmann, 25–73. Princeton: Princeton University Press, 1994.
Taylor, Charles. *Sources of the Self: The Making of the Modern Identity*. Cambridge: Cambridge University Press, 1989.
Torpey, John. *The Invention of the Passport: Surveillance, Citizenship and the State*. Cambridge: Cambridge University, 2000.
Van der Ploeg, Irma. 'Written on the Body: Biometrics and Identity'. *Computers and Society* 29:1 (1999): 37–44.
Velleman, J. David. 'Narrative Explanation'. *The Philosophical Review* 112 (2003): 1–25.
Watson, Ian. 'A Short History of National Identification Numbering in Iceland'. *Bifröst Journal of Social Science* 4 (2010): 51–89.
Weßels, Janna. 'Sexual Orientation in Refugee Status Determination'. Refugee Studies Centre, Working Paper Series No. 74. Oxford: University of Oxford, Department of International Development, 2011. Accessed 6 February 2017. http://www.refworld.org/pdfid/55c9fe604.pdf.
Wolfe, Matt. 'The Last Unknown Man'. *New Republic*, 21 November 2016 Accessed 30 May 2017. https://newrepublic.com/article/138068/last-unknown-man.
Wyman, Mark. *DPs: Europe's Displaced Persons, 1945–1951*. Ithaca and London: Cornell University Press, 1998.
Zureik, Elia and Mark D. Salter, *Global Surveillance and Policing, Borders, Security, Identity*. Cullompton: Willan Publishing, 2005.

Other

The Associated Press. 'Kissing Cousins? Icelandic App Warns You if Your Date Is a Relative'. *CBC.ca*, 18 April 2013. Accessed 1 June 2017, http://www.cbc.ca/news/business/kissing-cousins-icelandic-app-warns-if-your-date-is-a-relative-1.1390256.
Bielicki, Jan. 'Warum die Medien so spat über Köln berichteten'. *Süddeutsche Zeitung*, 7 January 2016. Accessed 24 March 2017. http://www.sueddeutsche.de/medien/uebergriffe-an-silvester-warum-die-medien-so-spaet-ueber-koeln-berichteten-1.2808386.
Brown, Nathan. 'Benjaman Kyle: A Man in Search of his Identity'. *Nuvo: Indy's Alternative Voice*, 1 March 2013. Accessed 16 February 2017. http://www.nuvo.net/indianapolis/benjaman-kyle-a-man-in-search-of-his-identity/Content?oid=2540059.

Bundeszentrale für politische Bildung. 'Film im NS-Staat'. Last updated 5 August 2013. Accessed 21 March 2017. http://www.bpb.de/geschichte/nationalsozialismus/geheimsache-ghettofilm/153344/film-im-ns-staat.

Busch, Christoph, Uwe Seidel, Olaf Henniger, Moazzam Butt, Christian Rathgeb, Jens Hermans, Günter Schumacher, Jan Löschner, Edward Springmann, Uwe Rabeler and Andreas Wolf. 'Trustworthy Lifecycle Management for Public Documents: A Proposal by the European Research Project FIDELITY in Collaboration with the EC JRC'. FIDELITY homepage (2014). Accessed 19 March 2017. http://www.fidelity-project.eu/media/White-Papers/FIDELITY_White-Paper_Trustworthy-lifecycle-management.pdf.

Dearden, Lizzie. 'German Solder Posing as Syrian Refugee Arrested for Planning "False Flag" Terror Attack'. *The Independent*, 27 April 2017. Accessed 31 May 2017. http://www.independent.co.uk/news/world/europe/german-soldier-syria-refugee-false-flag-terror-attack-posing-arrested-frankfurt-france-bavaria-a7705231.html

Domonoske, Camila. '17-Year-Old Transgender Boy Wins Texas Girls' Wrestling Championship'. *NPR.org*, 27 February 2017. Accessed 30 March 2017. http://www.npr.org/sections/thetwo-way/2017/02/27/517491492/17-year-old-transgender-boy-wins-texas-girls-wrestling-championship.

Finch, Suzanne. 'The Lie-Detecting Security Kiosk of the Future'. *SDSU NewsCenter*, 16 December 2016. Accessed 6 February 2017, http://newscenter.sdsu.edu/sdsu_newscenter/news_story.aspx?sid=76505.

Forsyth, Neil. 'Do You Know This Man?' *The Guardian*, 10 July 2010. Accessed 1 April 2016. http://www.theguardian.com/lifeandstyle/2010/jul/10/man-with-no-memory-america.

Friedman, Uri. 'Where American Terrorists Actually Come From'. *The Atlantic*, last updated 30 January 2017. Accessed 7 February 2017, https://www.theatlantic.com/international/archive/2017/01/trump-immigration-ban-terrorism/514361/.

Gorodnichy, Dmitry O., S. Eastwood, V. Shmerko, S. Yanushevich. 'Automated Border Control Systems as Part of e-Border Crossing Process'. NIST International Biometric Performance Conference (IBPC 2014). Accessed 1 June 2017. https://www.nist.gov/sites/default/files/documents/2016/12/01/14-nist-abc-eborder-gorodnichy.p.pdf

Hudak, Stephen. 'No-man's Land: Amnesia Stole His Identity for 11 Years'. *Orlando Sentinel*, 22 September 2015. Accessed 1 April 2016, http://www.orlandosentinel.com/news/local/os-benjamin-kyle-amnesia-identified-20150921-story.html.

Justice, Kent. 'Benjaman Kyle Writes "Thank You" Post: Man Learns his True Identity after 11 Years, Thanks Those Who Helped Him'. *News4Jax*, September 16, 2015. Accessed 30 May 2017. http://www.news4jax.com/news/benjamin-kyle-writes-thank-you-post.

Lambda Legal. 'Changing Birth Certificate Sex Designations: State-by-State Guidelines'. Last updated on 3 February 2015. Accessed on 17 March 2017. http://www.lambdalegal.org/know-your-rights/article/trans-changing-birth-certificate-sex-designations.

Laws of Malta (electronic repository provided by the Ministry for Justice, Culture and Local Government). *Gender Identity, Gender Expression, and Sex Characteristics*

Act, 14 April 2015. Accessed 17 March 2017. http://justiceservices.gov.mt/Down loadDocument.aspx?app=lom&itemid=12312&l=1.

Lewis, Daniel. 'Daniel J. Berrigan, Defiant Priest Who Preached Pacifism, Dies at 94'. *New York Times*, 30 April 2016. Accessed 21 March 2017. https://www.nytimes.com/2016/05/01/nyregion/daniel-j-berrigan-defiant-priest-who-preached-pacifism-dies-at-94.html?_r=0

Lowe, Derek. 'All Natural and Chemical Free'. Personal blog *In the Pipeline* 2 July 2014. Accessed 20 March 2017. http://blogs.sciencemag.org/pipeline/archives/2014/07/02/all_natural_and_chemical_free.

Matteucci, Megan. 'A Real Live Nobody'. *Savannah Morning News*, 24 September 2007. Accessed 1 April 2016. http://savannahnow.com/news/2007-09-24/real-live-nobody#.

MDR Sachsen-Anhalt. 'Entsetzen im Landtag über Poggenburg'. Last updated on 4 February 2017. Accessed on 19 March 2017. http://www.mdr.de/sachsen-anhalt/landespolitik/poggenburg-eklat-landtag-100.html

Medlock, Michael A. 'Second Chances' Season 6, Episode 24 of *Star Trek: The Next Generation* (1993), created by Gene Roddenberry.

Mische, George. 'Inattention to Accuracy about "Catonsville Nine" Distorts History'. *National Catholic Reporter*, published online 17 May 2013. Accessed 21 March 2017. https://www.ncronline.org/news/peace-justice/inattention-accuracy-about-catonsville-nine-distorts-history.

Parodi, Emilio and Antonella Cinelli, 'Berlin Truck Attack Suspect Shot Dead by Police in Italy'. *reuters.com*, 23 December 2016. Accessed 1 June 2017. http://www.reuters.com/article/us-germany-truck-idUSKBN14C0JP.

Politan, Vinnie, Kelly Krammes and Julie Wolfe. 'DNA Expert: Man without Identity Wants It That Way'. *11Alive Atlanta*, 5 February 2015. Accessed 16 February 2017. http://legacy.11alive.com/story/news/crime/2015/02/01/man-lives-for-decade-not-knowing-who-he-is/22583483/.

Rankin, Jennifer. 'European Parliament Set to Pass Passenger Data Law'. *The Guardian*, 13 April 2017. Accessed 19 March 2017. https://www.theguardian.com/world/2016/apr/13/european-parliament-set-to-pass-passenger-data-law.

Saner, Emine. 'Europe's Terrible Trans Rights Record: Will Denmark's New Law Spark Change?' *The Guardian*, 1 September 2014. Accessed 17 March 2017. https://www.theguardian.com/society/shortcuts/2014/sep/01/europe-terrible-trans-rights-record-denmark-new-law.

Schmall, Emily. 'Transgender Advocates Hail Law Easing Rules in Argentina'. *New York Times*, 24 May 2012. Accessed 17 March 2017. http://www.nytimes.com/2012/05/25/world/americas/transgender-advocates-hail-argentina-law.html

Skatteverket. 'Flytta till Sverige'. Accessed 23 March 2017. https://www.skatteverket.se/privat/folkbokforing/flyttatillsverige.4.76a43be412206334b89800018617.html

Social Security Administration. 'Identity Theft and Your Social Security Number'. Accessed 22 March 2017, https://www.ssa.gov/pubs/EN-05-10064.pdf.

United States Holocaust Memorial Museum. 'Antisemitic Legislation 1933–1939'. Accessed 2 February 2017, https://www.ushmm.org/wlc/en/article.php?ModuleId=10007901.

Wikstrom, John. *Finding Benjaman*. 2011. Available on *Vimeo*. Accessed 16 February 2016. https://vimeo.com/34589969.

Yuhas, Alan and Mazin Sidhamed. 'Is This a Muslim Ban? Trump's Executive Order Explained'. *The Guardian*, last updated 31 January 2017. Accessed 7 February 2017. https://www.theguardian.com/us-news/2017/jan/28/trump-immigration-ban-syria-muslims-reaction-lawsuits.

Index

Alternative für Deutschland (AfD), 99, 104
amnesia, 1–4, 13
Anderson, Benedict, 71–72
animalism. *See* personal identity: physical criteria of
anti-gay propaganda, 99–101, 105
anti-Semitism, 54, 99, 106–7
Ashkenazi Jews, 52–53

bathroom bills, 51, 105–6
bias. *See* trust: social trust
biometry, 43–44, 68–71, 95
birth certificates. *See* breeder documents
border control, 44, 47, 74–77, 85, 94–98, 107–8; American border control authorities, 100. *See also* Trump, Donald J.
border guards: virtual border guards, 110n21. *See also* border control
breeder documents, 44, 76, 85–86, 88–90, 93, 117–18
Brexit, 104

coherentism, 90–91
curriculum vitae (CV), 41, 43, 49

dementia, 21–22, 29n71, 41
depression, 46–47

displaced persons (DPs), 73–75
draft registries, 60–62

Emcke, Carolin, 98–99
epistemology, 32–33, 45–53, 87–93; social epistemology, 96, 110–11n23
EURODAC (European Dactyloscopy), 68–69. *See also* refugees; terrorism

forensics. *See* biometry
Foucault, Michel, 59–60, 68
foundationalism, 89–90

gender identity, 33–34, 51–52, 91–93, 118; and legal sex assignment, 51–53, 91–93; and sport, 33–34, 51–52, 55nn5–6
Goffman, Erving, 35, 42–43, 50
Guerre, Martin, 43, 64

Hume, David, 5, 7–8, 16–17, 38–40
hypocoristics, 63–64, 79n24

identity theft, 13–14, 43

Kant, Immanuel, 8, 16–19, 23, 38
Karolinska Institute (KI). *See* Macchiarini, Paolo
Kyle, Benjaman, 1–7, 13

Lindemann, Hilde, 8, 36, 40–46
Locke, John, 10, 16–17, 20
Luhmann, Niklas, 102–5

Macchiarini, Paolo, 49–51
MacIntyre, Alasdair, 34–37
maps, as expressions of nationalism, 72, 75, 78n8
misrecognition. *See* recognition
mistrust, 101–8

names. *See* hypocoristics; onomastics; patronymics
Nansen passports. *See* passports: issued to stateless refugees
narrative, 34–53, 86, 88, 116. *See also* epistemology; recognition
nationalism, 71, 98–100, 111n30
Nazi Germany. *See* anti-Semitism
nicknames. *See* hypocoristics

Olson, Eric, 20–21
onomastics, 62–64, 78–79n12, 79n20

Parfit, Derek, 5–6, 9–14, 16–17, 21, 23, 34–35
passenger name record (PNR), 94–95
passports, 47, 72–77, 93–94; biometric passports, 75–77; as brands, 71–75; issued to stateless refugees, 73
patronymics, 62–63
PEGIDA (Patriotische Europäer gegen die Islamisierung des Abendlandes), 104, 113n50
personal identity: and material and immaterial substances, 11, 18, 23; memory criterion of, 5, 10–11, 14 (*see also* amnesia); metaphysics of, 5–25, 116; and moral agency, 17–19; physical criteria of, 2–3, 11, 17–23, 27n37, 32–33, 43–44 (*see also* biometry). *See also* Hume, David; Kant, Immanuel; Locke, John; Parfit, Derek
personnummer (Swedish personal number), 64–70, 80n27, 80n29, 88
Polizeiwissenschaft, 59–60

postmodernism, 77
privacy, 66–67, 97
pronouns: Mühlhäusler and Harré's study of, 15, 23–25

Quante, Michael, 20–23

recognition, 4–8, 13–14, 31–37, 53–54, 56n15
refugees, 52–53, 69–70, 91, 99; gay refugees, 91

Schechtman, Marya, 8, 15, 35–40, 44, 53–54
science fiction, 9–13, 118
Scott, James C., 61, 67, 74–75, 116
security. *See* border control; terrorism
social security number, 2–3, 65
statelessness, 73–75. *See also* displaced persons; passports: issued to stateless refugees
Strawson, Galen, 37–41
surnames. *See* Ashkenazi Jews; onomastics; patronymics

Taylor, Charles (philosopher), 34–35
technologies of the self, 59–60, 68
terrorism, 52, 75–77, 99–100
torture, 53–54
transgender. *See* gender identity
Trump, Donald J., 99–100, 102, 104–5
trust, 94–108, 117; and emotion, 102; epistemic trust, 95, 97–98; e-trust, 96–98; function of, 66, 102; social trust, 96–98, 101–2 (*see also* epistemology: social epistemology); and trustworthy identification, 95–98, 101–2
truthiness, 106, 113n56

United States: history of the immigration policy of the, 113n54. *See also* Trump, Donald J.

Velleman, David, 50

Wittgenstein, Ludwig, 23

About the Author

Maren Behrensen is a post-doctoral researcher at the Institute for Christian Social Ethics at the University of Münster, Germany.

www.ingramcontent.com/pod-product-compliance
Lightning Source LLC
Chambersburg PA
CBHW021852300426
44115CB00005B/126